ARRESTED?

A Former Prosecutor's Guide To ~~Surviving~~ Thriving After Being Charged With A Crime

JOHN P. CANNON

CANNON & ASSOCIATES - YOUR FIERCE ADVOCATES®

Informed Criminal Defense

Copyright © 2023 by Cannon and Associates Law, PLLC

All rights reserved. No part of this publication may be reproduced, distributed, or transmitted in any form or by any means, including photocopying, recording, or other electronic or mechanical methods, without the prior written permission of the publisher, except in the case of brief quotations embodied in critical reviews and other non-commercial uses permitted by copyright law.

Please write to the publisher for permission requests, addressed: "Attention: Permissions Coordinator, at the address below."

PUBLISHING HOUSE

NightWriters Publishing

Ordering Info:

Cannon and Associates Law Firm, PLLC

Attn: John P. Cannon

401 North Hudson Avenue

Oklahoma City, Oklahoma 73102

Printed in United States of America

2nd Edition 2023

Cannon & Associates

DISCLAIMER

This publication is for informational purposes only. Nothing in this book constitutes legal advice for your specific situation. No attorney-client relationship is intended or in fact created by being provided a copy of this book or reading the materials contained in this book. The author assumes no liability for any errors, omissions, or detrimental reliance on material contained in this book. Please consult with an experienced criminal defense attorney or other appropriate expert for legal or other advice.

Cannon & Associates

Your Fierce Advocates®

401 North Hudson Avenue

Oklahoma City, OK 73102

(405) 657-2323

www.JPCannonLawFirm.com

FOREWORD

This book was written to help people, period. The book is primarily intended to help defendants and the families of defendants facing the criminal justice system. It would take many volumes to address every issue in the criminal justice system, and this book is not designed to accomplish that goal. Rather, this is intended to provide a snapshot of what you and your family will likely face going forward, whether your case is prosecuted at the federal, state, juvenile, municipal or military level.

This book is designed to address the most common questions faced by potential clients and families facing the widest range of the criminal justice system. It is not designed to answer every question about your specific case. In order to have questions answered about your specific situation, you need to meet with an experienced criminal defense attorney that has the discovery and all information relevant to your case. As we say, no two cases nor any two clients are exactly alike.

We'd be glad to meet with you for a confidential, no pressure strategy session to address questions and concerns about your case, and see if we are Your Fierce Advocates® before or after you read our book. Whatever you do, please find experienced counsel, it is an investment that may change the course of your life and future.

DEDICATION

I would like to dedicate this book to my family and my amazing staff of Your Fierce Advocates®. My family gives me the strength to get up every day and serve our clients and our community.

Additionally, I would like to thank the Oklahoma County Public Defender's Office that gave me, and some of the best defense attorneys in the state, the opportunity to fight for our clients in complex and interesting cases. All while maintaining professionalism and quality representation in difficult situations.

The years I spent as a public defender forged in me a desire to constantly serve my clients with compassion, and helped me build a firm of Your Fierce Advocates®.

All the adversity I've had in my life, all my troubles and obstacles, have strengthened me... You may not realize it when it happens, but a kick in the teeth may be the best thing in the world for you.

– Walt Disney

Informed Criminal Defense

TABLE OF CONTENTS

Testimonials

Section 1: FINDING YOUR FIERCE ADVOCATE® ....
- What Makes a Great Criminal Defense Law Firm?..................
- Myths of Arrest and Defense Attorneys...........................
- Can I Help my Attorney with My Case?............................
- Three Choices in Your Criminal Case............................

Section 2: BEGINNING OF YOUR CASE............................
- Arrest: The First 48 Hours.......................................
- Miranda Warnings...
- Release from Jail and Beyond....................................
- Bail and Bond in Oklahoma..
- Arraignment..

Section 3: STATE CRIMINAL DEFENSE............................
- State Court Proceedings Overview................................
- Factors in Going to Trial on Your Case..........................
- State Court Criminal Probation..................................
- Consequences of a Conviction....................................
- Diversion Programs...
- Common Crimes..
- Driving Under the Influence.....................................
- Youthful Offender..

Section 4: FEDERAL CRIMINAL DEFENSE..........................
- Federal Investigations..
- Federal Court Proceedings Overview..............................
- Federal Criminal Trial and Beyond...............................
- Federal Sentencing & Beyond.....................................

Section 5: MILITARY CRIMINAL DEFENSE.........................
- Military Defense Overview.......................................

Informed Criminal Defense
Military Administrative Proceedings..............................

CONCLUSION...

Your Fierce Advocates®..
Cannon & Associates – Set Apart......................................
Acknowledgments..
Testimonials..

CLIENT TESTIMONIALS

"I signed up with John June 25th, July 5th. I received an email that my case is in line to be DISMISSED, within a 2-week time period. John made what was one of the most stressful times in my life better! Every case is different, but he handled my case with care, and he was extremely open in his communication throughout the whole process. I hope to never have to have a criminal attorney again but if I do I will definitely go back to John. I highly recommend him to anyone else who is needing an attorney!"

Ashley

"John Cannon is an EXCELLENT attorney. He handled my case professionally and quickly. He is the first attorney I have ever met to take my situation and handle it without dragging it out occurring more expenses. I highly recommend him and will use him again if needed!"

Sarah

"Hands down the best lawyer. Mr. Cannon accepted my case and got on it the same day. I would give him 10 stars if I could. I really appreciate the dedication on how he handles things with a short time frame."

Chris

"John Cannon assisted me through a very difficult time in my military career. He worked tirelessly with me on my case and kept me informed during the entire process. I can't say enough good things about Mr. Cannon. He's incredibly knowledgeable with regards to military justice. The outcome of my case was successful, and I attribute that to Mr. Cannon's professionalism and expertise in dealing with military law. I would highly recommend Mr. Cannon to anyone with military justice or criminal defense needs."

Susan

"My attorney Mr. Tom Stone has went above and beyond to make sure all matters were taken care of. I stay about 5 hours away and he made sure to keep me updated through calls and other communications. His paralegal Ms. Brittany done an excellent job answering questions and making sure I could speak with Mr. Stone as needed. The whole team is very helpful, and they even have accommodating payment options. I give Cannon & Associates two thumbs up."

LaNesha

"The staff at Cannon and Associates will go out of their way every time to ensure you are taken care of and your mind is at ease. The hard work that Mr. Cannon, Angelia, and the team have put in for me allowed me to start my life again. They were always responsive to my inquiries and never left me out of the loop. Not once did I ever have to wonder what was going on. They fight for every client as if the world depended on it. I highly recommend this law firm to anyone who is seeking legal representation."

Jason G.

"They were amazing!!! My case was dismissed!! Mr. Jones went above and beyond and was super patient when i got emotional, he honestly cared!! I couldn't be more happy with my outcome!! I would definitely recommend them to anyone going through any kinda unfortunate events."

Carrie

"Mr. Cannon represented my husband on a case we were very concerned might not go our way. The next court date we were predicting my husband might not be coming home for a while. Not only did Mr. Cannon and his office team work quickly on the matter, they all were extremely informative and communicated well with us through the whole process. Once in court, Mr. Cannon communicated thoroughly with us, went over our options & possibilities, and didn't give up fighting for my husband's innocence. He was able to get the case dismissed for my husband. It was truly a blessing to have someone work hard for our family and care to make sure he stayed home with us. The office has been great working with us on payments in order for them to keep representing our case. Overall, we were beyond impressed with the work done and would highly recommend Mr. Cannon and his office for anyone needing a great attorney."

Stefanie T.

"I recently called Cannon & Associates seeking legal advice. All of my questions were well received and answered very knowledgeably by Kelly. The office is beautiful, everyone is very

respect and courteous, as well as extremely knowledgeable and professional. I would highly recommend this law firm to anyone."

Kasey Z.

~~~~~~

"I have nothing but good comments to make about Cannon and Associates. Attorneys John Cannon and Thomas Stone went to bat for me and the outcome was extraordinary. These guys listened to my situation, conducted excellent discovery and appeared before the judge with me in court. I must give my God the glory and praise. I believe John and Thomas used their skills and experience via God's oversight and intervention. I highly recommend this firm and these attorneys."

Art

~~~~~~

"Outstanding law firm, their experience with military law and the civilian sector is the best I have worked with. Professional office, amazing staff and overall, just amazing people that will go the distance for their clients. They care about their people and in getting the best outcome they can for their clients. Recommend as the #1 office in OKC and Edmond."

Ben

SECTION ONE: FINDING YOUR FIERCE ADVOCATE®

[QR code: FINDING YOUR FIERCE ADVOCATE]

"When I called Cannon & Associates my husband and I had given up hope that anyone in the justice system would help us, but John and his staff restored our faith in good people! They are kind and HONEST and we did NOT feel judged ever. They are our angels. From the first phone call to the prompt action and kindness they showed us at his court date John and Regina have been amazing. John makes no promises or exaggerations. He is honest and tells the truth about our situation. We have never doubted we had the best chance with John. I could write pages about how impressed and grateful we have been since he took our case. They care about your story and provide education about the court process every step of the way. You will never be left wondering what is going on or what will happen next. They lay it out for you from the moment you call, and everything happens exactly the way they say it will!!"

Emily

WHAT MAKES A GREAT CRIMINAL DEFENSE LAW FIRM?

"Wonderful firm. They helped us get through a difficult spot. Very responsive, thorough, and always on top of things. Tom was amazing and put us at ease right away and always made sure we were aware of what was happening and when."

Diana

Your Fierce Advocates® in the criminal division of Cannon & Associates only defend Citizens and Soldiers facing criminal charges. We are not a general practice firm. We specialize in criminal defense to ensure you receive the best representation possible. You should hire a law firm that only handles a few areas of practice, with substantial experience in criminal defense. You should only hire a law firm with attorneys that have existing, positive, professional relationships with the individuals they come in contact with on your behalf in your case.

The law firm you hire should not only have years of experience, but years of handling complex and challenging criminal defense cases across the state and at every level of the criminal justice system. Many attorneys have decades of experience, but how many years have they practiced criminal defense? How many criminal defense cases do they handle every year? How many criminal defense cases have they handled in their career? How many criminal jury trials have they conducted? Were they first or second chair attorney in those cases? Your case and your future are in better hands with a Law Firm and an attorney that has handled the cases of over 1,000 criminal defendants across the spectrum of criminal justice. Cannon & Associates is that law firm.

There are pros and cons to the accessibility of online marketing in today's legal market. An attorney can get substantial exposure without the experience necessary to competently defend individuals facing serious charges; however, if you look hard enough you will find the truth about their experience and expertise. You want a law firm and attorney visible online with a professional website, but your research should not stop there. Seek out and view their reviews, YouTube channel, their written and video blogs, their social media posts, and the testimonials of their former clients.

You will be starting with a disadvantage if you hire a criminal defense law firm without a great reputation. The business organization of the law firm you retain is crucial to your success. When cases and clients stack up or trial is upon them, a law firm with procedures will efficiently stay on top of all their clients' cases, a disorganized law firm will not. There is no faster way to learn about the character and caliber of your potential attorney than former client reviews and testimonials.

You will be better served by hiring an attorney with a large number of good-to-great reviews than an attorney with only three or four perfect scores. Attorney recognition matters to lawyers, and it should matter to you as a potential client. Has the attorney you are considering received peer-reviewed awards? Is there a vetting process for the awards he/she has received? Attorney awards function similar to other professions, so pay attention. The absence of any awards may be a reason to consider continuing your search for your attorney.

Some law firms undercut competing firms, regardless of the true value or cost to defend a specific type of case. You want to hire a

Informed Criminal Defense

law firm that is happy to represent you, but does not 'need' your business. Hiring a criminal defense attorney can be a confusing and sometimes scary experience. When you or a loved one's future and' freedom hang in the balance it is crucial you retain the right counsel. The best way to address this concern is by doing your homework: seek opinions, read reviews, visit websites, interview law firms, and trust your gut. Meet a few firms and hire the best criminal defense law firm you can afford.

This is one of the most important decisions you will make, do not take it lightly. Hiring the attorney with the lowest price is never good for your case or future. You get what you pay for in criminal defense law firms, as with many things in life. Observe the law firm you consider hiring, how they conduct business will be indicative of how they will handle your case, your future, and your life.

MYTHS OF ARREST AND DEFENSE ATTORNEYS

"John and his staff are great! John helped me through a difficult case I thought but John got done for me what 3 other attorneys couldn't. John kept in constant contact and even made appearances for me when I couldn't. He's a very caring and understanding person. Thanks so much Cannon and Associates for all your help in resolving the matter. Excellent team!"

Chris

This chapter was written to address some of the most common myths those facing criminal charges and their families have about arrest and hiring a criminal defense attorney. Often clients tell me during our first meeting they have already spoken to police and given their side of the story, or waited to hire an attorney because they did not want to appear guilty.

More often than not, these actions do more harm than good. The following are myths we see or hear about on a regular basis. Hopefully, you will not make the same mistake so many have before you. Whether you did or not, you can still assist in your defense by being proactive and working with an experienced defense attorney, no matter what has happened in the past.

MYTH 1: HIRING AN EXPERIENCED CRIMINAL DEFENSE ATTORNEY MAKES YOU LOOK GUILTY

Many myths exist concerning being arrested for an alleged crime, and about hiring a criminal defense attorney. The most common myth about criminal defense attorneys is that hiring one makes you look guilty. This could not be farther from the truth. Police, prosecutors, and judges assume nothing more than you know your rights and you are exercising them when you hire an experienced criminal defense attorney.

If you know a law enforcement officer or attorney, ask them, if they would hire an attorney, if under investigation; they would be the first to tell you they will not speak to law enforcement without an attorney, and they would hire an experienced attorney to help them in their circumstance.

MYTH 2: ALL CRIMINAL DEFENSE ATTORNEYS ARE EQUAL

Another popular myth, all criminal defense attorneys are the same. However, experience, knowledge, and reputation matter with criminal defense attorneys just as with every other profession. An experienced criminal defense attorney has faced seasoned prosecutors and knows the tactics they will implement in your case.

It takes experience to know how to evaluate the strengths and weaknesses in the prosecutor's case in order to advise a client about his/her prospects at trial. Additionally, you want an experienced litigator that has tried cases with success, if you need to fight your case. Experience never matters more than when your freedom is on the line.

MYTH 3: ANY ATTORNEY CAN DEFEND A CRIMINAL CASE

Another common myth is that any attorney can defend a criminal case. A personal injury lawyer is not capable of handling an antitrust case, just as a civil attorney is not the best choice for your criminal defense. Defending criminal clients in State and Federal court is an art, which requires experience specific to criminal law and skills, which are developed overtime and experience.

MYTH 4: YOU CAN CLEAR YOUR NAME WITH POLICE

Myth. Many people accused of a crime want to immediately clear their name; they are wrong. It is important to present your side of the case; however, it is best to exercise this right with the assistance of experienced criminal defense counsel. Often, a client will speak to police and corroborate or confirm some or all aspects of a charge they are facing without even knowing what they have done. Law enforcement can present charges to the prosecution on any crime they have probable cause to believe you or your loved one have committed. You should help your attorney defend your case; not help the police prosecute your case.

MYTH 5: PUBLIC DEFENDERS ARE NOT GOOD LAWYERS

Public Defenders are not good lawyers; myth. As a former public defender, I have first-hand knowledge of the fact that Public Defenders are often dedicated and highly skilled attorneys, who choose to dedicate all or part of their career to public service. Public Defenders work solely in criminal defense, and although they have very large dockets, they are often very dedicated to their clients.

However, many of them are brand new attorneys, have limited trial practice, and overwhelming dockets. You cannot control the Public Defender assigned to your case. You cannot know, if you will be assigned an experienced Public Defender or not; however, you can control, which attorney you hire.

MYTH 6: POLICE HAVE TO TELL SUSPECTS THE TRUTH

Many people believe police are required to tell the truth; this is a myth. Police are allowed to lie and misrepresent facts during the course of an investigation. In fact, it is one of the most effective investigative techniques used. I would not mention it here, if it rarely occurred. Police have a job to investigate crime, but you are not required to make their job easier. You have the right to remain silent, exercise it.

CAN I HELP MY ATTORNEY WITH MY CASE?

"I would highly recommend Cannon & Associates to anyone who is looking for a professional, compassionate, and very knowledgeable attorney. John was not only extremely polite, but he always responded to my questions or concerns in a timely manner. His office staff is very nice, and they were always extremely helpful. I am satisfied with the way he handled my case and how he explained it very well during each step. Thank you, John, for everything! Hopefully I don't ever need you again but if I ever do, I definitely know who to contact! :)"

Belen

Yes, you can help your attorney. There are many things you can do throughout the process of your case to help your criminal defense attorney defend you. The biggest and sometimes hardest step is to listen to and trust your selected counsel. You must use due diligence in selecting your criminal defense attorney; for one, so that you can be confident in following their advice.

What Can I Do Between Court Dates?

Many clients rightfully want to do everything they can to help their cause between court dates. I appreciate and encourage clients to be proactive, with the disclaimer you should only do things for

Informed Criminal Defense

your case that you have consulted with your criminal defense attorney about previously.

Counseling: After consulting with your criminal defense attorney, seeking counseling is potentially a positive step to take to help your case. Counseling for an issue identifiable in your case or personal life can be of great benefit, such as: substance abuse, alcohol abuse, mental health, emotional health issues. Additionally, if you are seeking to resolve your case with a plea agreement, counseling may be a condition of probation, which you get out of the way by completing while your case is pending.

Prosecutors and judges look very favorably on defendants that take steps to address concerns or to simply better themselves. Taking steps to address an issue you or your attorney identify cannot be used against you in court. It is considered a remedial measure to address a concern and is not admissible to prove guilt.

Community Service: After consulting with your criminal defense attorney, completing community service (working for free!) may be beneficial to your case. Again, prosecutors and judges look favorably upon defendants that try to help out in their community. Further, community service will likely be a condition of probation and you can complete this condition, while your case is pending.

Volunteering your time and energy to a good cause, such as a shelter, food bank, or non-profit organization, if you have time outside of work or school, is looked highly upon by prosecutors and judges alike. Volunteering helps illustrate an important narrative of caring about your community and your dedication to getting past the current situation.

Alcoholics Anonymous & Narcotics Anonymous: similar to counseling, attending NA or AA meetings can not only have a positive effect on your life, but a positive effect on your case. Your criminal defense attorney does not have to disclose to the prosecutor that you are attending these meetings, but it is a useful tool for your attorney to be able to reference the good work you are doing.

Complete tasks: An experienced criminal defense attorney, in the right circumstance, will give you tasks to complete while your case is pending. Upon consulting with your attorney, you may be tasked to write a statement, take photographs of a location, get contact information for witnesses (that are not victims or prosecution witnesses), and many other potential tasks. It is important to speak to your attorney before investigating your case, as discussed previously. You should take an active role in your case, as long as you are on the same page as your attorney.

Biography: Your attorney can only articulate your life story if he or she knows it. Every client that hires Cannon & Associates is asked to put together an autobiography of the good things and the hard things that have happened in their life. It does not have to be a long story, just a page or two, but part of your criminal defense attorney's job is to tell the human side of your story, which should soften the only story the prosecutor knows.

You can collect photographs for your attorney of different accomplishments or highlights of your life. In one case, my client's photographs of before and after suffering from methamphetamine use resulted in the prosecution agreeing to his being placed on probation with treatment as opposed to going to prison for many years. Stories matter in criminal defense, and no one can help your attorney tell your story better than you.

What Can I Do to Prepare My Case for Sentencing?

In Oklahoma, before any sentencing hearing you are entitled to and should exercise the right to a Pre-Sentence Investigation (PSI). You should prepare for this part of the process just as you have throughout your case, with continued communication between you and your attorney, and preparing what to say and how to say it. Sentencing is an opportunity for you and your defense attorney to tell your story, beyond the circumstance that led to your being arrested and charged with a crime. The life you are creating or have created while your case is pending is powerful if you are making changes in your life.

Informed Criminal Defense

Our team of Fierce Advocates® is dedicated to helping you build a plan to create a better future for you beyond your case. When you work with the right defense team, it is easy to build a plan for putting yourself and your case in the best light to seek the best outcome possible at sentencing. Prosecutors and judges see hundreds of cases and defendants. However, they do not see many people that take active steps to better themselves during the process. When you do some or all of the following, you stand out and increase the likelihood of better outcomes in your case:

- Obtain or maintain employment;
- Enroll or continue in education or vocational training;
- Obtain counseling services for any issues identified in your case;
- Get involved in treatment options for substance of alcohol abuse;
- Get assessments done to identify what, if any issues you are facing that you may or may not be aware of in your life. *This is exceedingly important, as you can be proactive in making improvements to yourself during your case, if you can identify the services you need!*
- Volunteer / give back to the community by either performing community service or completing community projects;
- Complete the statutory terms of probation, prior to sentencing. Nothing impresses prosecutors and judges more than someone that is proactive in getting the work done in their case; and
- Work with an experienced criminal defense attorney to identify the steps you should take in your specific circumstance to set yourself up for success

This list is long and may seem overwhelming; but not every step in the list above will apply to your case. However, we wanted to provide you with an idea of the many steps you can take to improve your chances for the best outcome in your case.

THREE CHOICES IN CRIMINAL CASE

"Mr. Cannon was efficient at getting a great result for my DUI client and showed compassion through the whole process which helped get the client through an unexpected and difficult situation. I highly recommend trusting him to handle your sensitive criminal defense needs."

Evan

Every criminal case, in every jurisdiction, at some point comes down to deciding between *three choices*. What each of three choices looks like will differ greatly based on the criminal system your case is in, as well as the specific court in which you appear. However, you will always be entitled to a version of each of these three choices:

1. **Fight your Case;**
2. **Reach an Agreement with the Prosecutor; or**
3. **Let the Court Determine the Outcome.**

1. Fight Your Case

Fighting your case is your constitutional right, regardless of the jurisdiction in which you find yourself. The government or prosecutor bears the burden of proof / is required to convince the fact finder, that you are guilty or culpable in your case. Therefore, you can hold the prosecutor to the burden of proof and force them to make their case to the judge or the jury.

In addition to your constitutional right to a jury trial, motion practice is a vital tool in your toolbox of three choices, which falls under the option to fight your case. You may raise legal, procedural, and factual arguments to the court or party responsible for deciding important legal questions in your case.

The timing and strategy behind each of these decisions is important and will be specific to whatever court your case is before. In federal court, the timeline is very fast and you must make these decisions quickly; however, you and your federal criminal defense attorney will have total access to the prosecution's evidence early on in the case. In state court criminal proceedings, motion practice happens often, but it is regularly later on in the case, after you have received discovery from the prosecutor, which can take longer than in federal court. Conversely, in the military justice process, the appropriateness of motions being filed will be dictated by a scheduling order or common practice within a specific command.

Prior to resolving your case through one of the other "choices" in every criminal case, it is important that you and your criminal defense attorney discuss the choice to fight your case or a specific issue in your case. Fighting may not be the best option in your criminal case; however, you should always consider holding the prosecution to its burden and evaluate the strength of the prosecution's case against you prior to entering a plea or giving up the right to hold them to their burden.

2. Reach an Agreement with the Prosecutor

Over 97% percent of cases in every criminal justice system in Oklahoma are resolved without trial

Informed Criminal Defense

Let that sink in for a moment... Now to be fair, many of those cases are resolved by dismissal, when you and your criminal defense attorney exercise your rights under the first choice, "fighting your case". However, the majority of criminal cases are resolved by some form of a plea agreement between the defendant and the prosecutor.

When you work with an experienced criminal defense team, you will be able to put yourself and your circumstance in the best light possible to present your case and your future to the prosecution. Taking steps to better yourself and address any issues you are experiencing will only help you obtain a better outcome. *See our information on Helping My Case.*

Most prosecutors are reasonable people; however, they need information from your criminal defense attorney and you in order to see you as "more than a case number and a criminal history." Almost all prosecutors, regardless of the system they operate in, have too many cases. Therefore, they lack the bandwidth to do a deep analysis of every case on their docket (cases they are assigned to handle for their office). Trust me, I'm a former prosecutor.

When you work with your prosecutor to build a compelling story of your life, circumstances, and your plan for the future, it will almost certainly result in a better offer to resolve your case. You should never feel forced to accept a plea deal or resolve your case without fighting; however, in many circumstances with the right offer in hand, it is a better choice than exercising your right to trial.

You have more control over this outcome than you know, so be proactive, work with your criminal defense team and **build the narrative of your life and plans for the future.** The story of your life and your circumstances are unique to you and that information matters. An experienced criminal defense attorney can make serious improvements to your circumstances when you help them tell a compelling story.

3. Let the Court Determine the Outcome

Whether the third choice, letting the "Court determine the outcome" is a good option or not, is highly dependent upon the specific court you find yourself in.

In state criminal court proceedings, many diversion options exist that fall under this third "choice." In diversion programs, you agree to participate in the program and the Court determines what your participation and requirements look like in order to successfully complete the program. The larger county courts have more options when it comes to diversion; however, nearly every state court in Oklahoma has at least one diversion option to consider.

Diversion options are typically more time consuming than probation. However, if or when you successfully complete the program, your case will be dismissed in most instances. Diversion options in state court criminal proceedings are designed to be a last resort to stop someone from being sent to prison. Although, some of our clients elect to participate in diversion programs to avoid felony convictions as well.

The most common diversion options are discussed elsewhere in the following chapters. However, it is important to note the most common options here: Drug Court, DUI court, Mental Health Court, Female Diversion, Veteran's Diversion, Veteran's Court, and Community Sentencing.

The other half of the "third choice" involves blind pleas. The term blind plea is self-explanatory. You enter a plea and you are blind to the outcome. In blind pleas, the court has full authority to decide the outcome or sentence; however, the court must first consider all the evidence and/or information presented by the parties before deciding the outcome.

You should think long and hard about your options before exercising your right to a blind plea. In state court proceedings, blind pleas are typically reserved for the situation in which you have done everything possible to reach a positive agreed plea in your case; however, the prosecutor is unwilling to make you an offer that you want to accept. In this instance, you enter a blind plea with the desire the court will give you a better deal or outcome than the prosecutor was willing to offer.

In federal criminal cases, all pleas could be characterized as blind pleas. When you work with an experienced federal criminal defense attorney, you should have a good sense of the likely outcome. However, the parties do not reach plea "deals" as they often do in state court criminal proceedings. Rather, the parties may agree on the sentencing range or charges in the Indictment that the defendant will plea; however, the federal District Judge conducting sentencing in your case will determine the sentence, not the parties.

Federal sentencing is an entirely different animal from state court criminal proceedings. Yet, you can still reach a very favorable outcome with the option of allowing the Court to decide the outcome of your case, if you are unsuccessful in exercising the first choice, fighting your case.

In military justice actions, you can allow the military judge to determine the outcome of your case, or the commander in some circumstances. In fact, this may be a good option to explore, if you are unable to reach a favorable outcome with the judge advocate prosecuting your case, or want to simply seek the mercy of your commander.

CONCLUSION: DECIDING BETWEEN YOUR THREE CHOICES

Whatever part of the criminal justice system you find yourself in, it is important to recognize that you have options/choices in your matter. Whether you decide to work with us or not, please ensure you have a firm understanding of the "Three Choices" available to you in your specific case (discussed above) and the following:

A. **What each choice means in your circumstance;**
B. **What the potential consequences/benefits are with each choice; and**
C. **The timeline to exercise each choice available to you**

With a firm understanding of this information for your case, you will be better situated to face the justice system than most criminal defendants.

SECTION TWO: IN THE BEGINNING OF YOUR CRIMINAL CASE

[QR code: BEGINNING OF YOUR CASE]

"Words cannot express how grateful our family is for making time to advise and represent our son. Our son was a suspect of a crime of which he was falsely accused and was asked to visit with law enforcement. Without John we would not have known how to navigate the process of a law enforcement interview. A very scary thing and something none of us in the family knew how to handle. On short notice (less than 24 hours before the interview) John agreed to meet with our family and attend the interview with our son. In short, the interview was a success, and the falsity of the accusations were uncovered. Without John and his advice who knows how the interview would have gone. John is a kind, compassionate, and wise lawyer with a heart for doing the right thing."

Phillip

ARREST: THE FIRST 48 HOURS

"Called basically panicking and they very kindly took the time to talk to my wife and I and calm us down by explaining everything. I very much look forward to working with Mr. Cannon and Associates to beat this case."

Anthony

There are few experiences more confusing and frightening than being placed in handcuffs and taken to jail. However, the fact that you or a loved one has been arrested means very little in your criminal defense. Your decisions and actions after being arrested mean far more than the fact you have been taken into custody. Law enforcement need very little evidence or information, in order to place someone under arrest, but the government needs far more in order to obtain a conviction.

Upon Book-In, the police department or other law enforcement agency will notify the detention center (county jail) of the recommended charges, which are often highly exaggerated, and bond/bail is set based on a schedule determined by the District Court. Once bail is set by schedule, you may post your complete bail, a cash bond. which you/your family will have returned to you at the conclusion of your case. Alternatively, you can hire a bail bond company, a bondsman, to post the amount, and you will be required to pay the company a percentage of your total bond. Most bond companies require 10% of your bond, which the company will keep at the conclusion of your case. One wrinkle in this

Informed Criminal Defense

process can come from having charges or holds in more than one county, which an attorney can address for you.

Those individuals that do not post bond, either by cash or a bondsman, will stay in jail until released by the Court, or will be in custody until an attorney can seek an agreement on conditional bond, which does not require money in order to be released, or to have your bond reduced.

What Happens After I Get to Jail?

Once you get to jail, you will be held until you can be "booked" into the jail. The booking process is administrative, takes many hours, and can be upsetting. However, do not lose hope. The fact you are booked into jail is more administrative than proof that you will remain in jail.

During booking you will have your property inventoried and placed in jail property. Your background will be evaluated by the jail, as well as a record search will conduct to see, if you have any warrants. Any other history will be considered by the jail/sheriff, and your housing/location in the jail will be determined by this information as well as space in the jail and your presumed charges for arrest.

You will likely have your picture taken and you will be fingerprinted during booking. Once all administrative tasks have been completed at the jail and your cell location is determined, you will be moved to the main body of the jail.

In larger counties, such as Oklahoma and Tulsa County, you may be placed in a pod with individuals with serious violent charges or even individuals that have been in jail for well over a year. It is important to prepare yourself mentally for confinement, whether you are in custody for a couple hours or during the life of your case.

Phone Calls in Jail

Do not say anything about your case over the jail phone. Every word you say on a jail call is recorded and can be accessed by investigators and prosecutors.

EVERY WORD YOU SAY ON JAIL CALLS IS RECORDED, LISTENED TO BY PROSECUTORS, AND WILL BE USED AGAINST YOU IN COURT TO HURT YOUR CASE. DO NOT SAY ANYTHING ABOUT YOUR CASE OVER THE PHONE.

After being arrested, your family or loved ones that you call will be curious about what happened or why you were arrested. It is very important that you do not speak about the substance of your case. Rather, ask them to post your bond/get you out of jail and begin your search for an experienced criminal defense attorney. I cannot overstate the fact that you cannot discuss your case over the phone, while in jail or otherwise. The call is recorded, and the prosecutors are listening.

We recommend you immediately research and find an experienced Oklahoma criminal defense attorney as soon as possible. Whether we are the right fit for your family or not, it is vital to success in your case that you hire the right defense attorney as soon as possible.

Hiring a criminal defense attorney as a suspect, during the investigation, or before arrest maximizes your opportunity to minimize your exposure. A hired criminal defense attorney can contact the law enforcement agency investigating you and possibly stop the process, or help you avoid arrest or prosecution.

Alternatively, if arrest is inevitable, your criminal defense attorney may be able to facilitate the time, date, and place you go into custody or assist in scheduling a walk-through, where you show up at jail, get processed, and leave immediately (*See Bond in Oklahoma Chapter*).

This small amount of control can provide a great amount of peace of mind for someone anticipating arrest. Your attorney can contact the prosecutor, and appear before the judge assigned to your case, if a warrant is pending, and seek to have your case placed on the docket (receive a court date) without going into custody at all.

Common Errors after Arrest

Time heals all wounds, except being charged with a criminal offense. Often, time is the enemy of your criminal defense, as the longer you are in custody, the greater the opportunity to make mistakes. Everything you state on jail calls is recorded and can be used against you. Additionally, the longer your case is pending the greater the risk of your stating something damaging to your case. The advent and spread of social media have resulted in hundreds, if not thousands of admissions and damaging statements being introduced against criminal defendants in Oklahoma. Whether you hire an experienced criminal defense attorney or not, be smarter than advertising admissions to a crime.

Talking about your case is the most common error criminal defendants make after being arrested. Phone calls are recorded in jail and used against defendants by the prosecution every day.

Conversations can be recorded in Oklahoma, if one party consents to the recording. What does that mean? A person on their own accord or with assistance of police can choose to record a conversation with you, and turn that information/recording over to the prosecution or police. You should speak to no one on earth except your attorney about your case, period.

Does Hiring an Attorney Make Me Look Guilty?

Hiring an attorney is simply the smart exercise of a Constitutional right, to anyone associated with your case. You have Rights, you should use them. Police/law enforcement are far less likely to attempt to coerce a confession out of you or a loved one, if you are represented by counsel.

Police know they cannot use a confession by someone represented by counsel, if the individual is detained and questioned without their attorney being present.

Regardless of your status of having hired a criminal defense attorney or not, you should never speak to law enforcement without your attorney present.

Once you have been arrested, your greatest defense is working with a skilled criminal defense attorney that has a team to support your case. Yes, there is a cost associated with hiring an experienced criminal defense attorney; however, it is an investment in your future and your freedom, which you cannot put a price on.

The first 48 hours after you are arrested will be scary, but breathe… take a moment… think with your brain, not with fear… and get to work addressing the road ahead.

WHAT ARE MY MIRANDA RIGHTS?

"I have gotten two felonies lowered to one misdemeanor, and the state is offering probation instead of jail. I cannot thank Mr. Cannon and everyone at his office enough, they have been very patient with me. I'm glad I called this office; it was truly a God send. Mr. Cannon is EXTREMELY knowledgeable and knows how to make things happen."

Tyron

In the previous chapter, we looked at the consequences of being arrested or interrogated without having first hired an experienced criminal defense attorney. These issues have teeth in your criminal case, based on the Supreme Court decision in *Miranda v. Arizona*, 384 U.S. 436 (1966), in which the Supreme Court decided statements in limited circumstances are not admissible against criminal defendants, despite how damaging the information may be to your defense.

There is a common misconception that Miranda Rights have a larger application than they in fact do. Information gained by interrogation which violates the requirements of Miranda may be used against an individual in their investigation; however, the words a suspect or criminal defendant say cannot be introduced at trial against the individual.

Although the application of Miranda is limited; the remedy is clear cut, suppression. That means the prosecutor cannot present these statements to the judge or jury, if suppressed. In order to prove cause for suppression, two requirements must be met: you must be in custody, i.e. a reasonable person would not feel free to leave and you are subject to interrogation.

Interrogation is a legal term of art in this context and does not cover all manner of statements police hear. Anything you say can and will be used against you if you offer the information freely.

Understanding the legal issues and nuisances of your Miranda Rights and its application to the facts of your case will either result in admission or suppression of evidence that will impact the outcome of your case. You do not need to know all the laws related to Miranda; however, you do need to work with a criminal defense firm that understands the law and that can fight for your rights.

You and your criminal defense attorney will certainly have the opportunity to speak prior to you making the decision, on whether or not you should speak to law enforcement or the prosecutor. The Founding Fathers believed in your right to remain silent, and our Supreme Court has recognized its importance ever since then. Exercise your Constitutional rights and meet with an experienced criminal defense attorney before making any statements.

JAIL RELEASE AND BEYOND

"I got my first criminal case in my life. I had no idea what to expect and was extremely scared. I chose this firm because Regina was amazing, I called crying and she reassured me everything was going to be OK. John was amazing as well very patient and understanding. My case got dismissed. He is very professional always got back to me fast. I would absolutely refer this firm."

Shannon

Although getting out of jail is a welcomed change in circumstance, it is far from the end of the road in your journey. If you are fortunate enough to get released on bail, a number of important things happen during your release: 1) your property is returned to you (unless kept as evidence), 2) your bondsman or the sheriff's department will give you a bail slip detailing your bond, booking charges, and your initial court date.

It is very important that you appear or have your attorney appear on your behalf, if allowed by the Court, to your initial court date, or your arraignment date. The date your arraignment will take place depends on whether or not you are in custody or out of custody. A date you were given prior to release from custody can change and it is important to stay in contact with your criminal defense attorney and bondsman to ensure you appear on the right date and do not miss your arraignment.

In many instances your charges, if any, will not be filed by the arraignment date you were given at jail. The arraignment date you initially receive is only a tentative date, which will change, if charges have not been filed yet. You cannot be arraigned on charges that aren't filed!

Whether or not you will be prosecuted for any offense, resulting in arrest or not, is decided by prosecutors, not police. The volume of cases and investigations plays a role in the delay between arrest and charges being filed, which can benefit you, if you retain an experienced criminal defense attorney. The prosecutor will not know your version of events, unless your attorney is able to communicate them to the prosecutor, hopefully prior to charges being filed.

It is important to keep track of your arraignment or first court date, and appear, unless you have hired an attorney and he/she advises otherwise. Failing to appear for your arraignment may result in a warrant being issued and your bond being increased or even denied.

Charges on Bail Slip

The charges listed on your bail slip are important. Although police or law enforcement cannot file criminal charges in court against you, the charges they recommend to prosecutors are often very close to what the prosecuting office actually files against you in District Court. Understanding your potential charges and the range of punishment for those charges will help prepare you for your defense.

After you have been released, take a few hours to be with loved ones; go home; take a shower; and relax for a few hours – Then, begin your research for an experienced, quality, criminal defense attorney. Look at attorneys' websites, written work, and what former clients say about their attorneys. You should not take the process lightly; it is key to your future that you hire an experienced criminal defense attorney.

We are proud to say that we have more 5-Star Google Reviews than 99% of lawyers in Oklahoma; however, that by itself does not mean we are the right fit for you and your family. It is

Informed Criminal Defense

important to work with an experienced criminal defense attorney to assist you in understanding the charges on your bail slip and initiate your defense strategy.

When you have a good idea of what you may be facing once prosecutors file your charges, your defense attorney can begin to develop a targeted defense for your case.

WHAT SHOULD YOU NOT DO AFTER GETTING OUT OF JAIL?

"Everyone in the office was very accommodating and Mr. Cannon was a consummate professional. I retained him to assist me with a pretty minor issue all things considered, but he never made me feel less than important. John and his staff were all quick to address any concerns I had and really helped me through a stressful time. Highly recommend."

Dusten

When you get out of jail, you should *not* investigate your own case. I repeat, **do not investigate your own case**. Criminal defendants have found themselves facing serious charges of intimidating and threatening witnesses for taking it upon themselves to investigate their own case, *even when your questions or research are completely innocent.*

Second, do not get arrested or pick up a new criminal case. Everything is not lost based on being arrested and potentially charged with a crime, even a serious crime. However, you will make it more difficult for yourself, and your defense attorney, if you get yourself into more trouble after you are released. The fewer criminal charges you are facing, the higher the likelihood an experienced criminal defense attorney can accomplish a favorable outcome in your case.

Informed Criminal Defense

Next, do not hire an attorney inexperienced in criminal defense for the type of charges you are facing. It is not important to hire an attorney that markets their work in criminal defense: it is important to hire an attorney experienced and talented in criminal defense. Your future and your freedom are far more important than the cost of investing in your defense. When you work with the right criminal defense attorney, you will increase your chances for a favorable outcome in your case.

When you get out of jail, do not ignore the problem of having looming criminal charges. Do not stop with going home and relaxing. Do your homework. Research, interview, and hire an experienced criminal defense attorney. Your future and freedom depend on your being proactive and hiring the right criminal defense lawyer.

BAIL AND BOND IN OKLAHOMA

"Mr. Cannon has represented me on 2 criminal cases and one civil case over the past 4 years. He has always served me honestly, speedily and with good moral direction. John has integrity and humility. He has never belittled me or treated me in an unfair manor. I appreciate all that he has done for me, and I most certainly recommend him to family, strangers and friends. I will definitely use Mr. Cannon in the future for any and all of my family's legal matters."

Candice

Although every misdemeanor and felony crime in Oklahoma is an arrestable offense, they also carry the presumption of bond. When an offense carries bond, it means you can get out of jail while your case is pending, if you or a bondsman posts your bond. You, your family, or a loved one can post a "Cash Bond" by directly going to the jail or courthouse and post the cash for your bond with a cashier's check or cash.

Some form of bond must be posted in almost every criminal case in Oklahoma. Those facing criminal charges are not simply released and asked to return to court on their promise to appear. The purpose of bond is two-fold. The first purpose of bond is to ensure the safety of the community. The second purpose of bond is to ensure criminal defendants appear in court.

Bond and Safety to the Community

The risk of someone posing a threat to the safety of the community is presumed to be higher after someone is arrested for a crime, as some courts presume the person is guilty for purposes of bond. Additionally, the more serious the offense you are arrested for, the greater the presumed risk of your posing a threat to the community. This is a major factor explaining why courts set bond very high in violent cases and repeat DUI offense cases; however, the bond may be very low in non-violent felonies.

Although the Court may set your bond at an initial amount that is too high for you and your family to post, your criminal defense attorney can certainly advocate for a bond reduction that may allow your family to post bond in your case. An experienced criminal defense attorney may be able to present a compelling argument to the Court to convince the judge that you are not a threat to the safety of the community or yourself, and that your bond should be reduced to a reasonable amount.

Bond and Flight Risk

The other primary factor in Courts setting bond is flight risk, or the threat of someone not returning for court. It is assumed that for very serious cases or cases with a high likelihood of conviction, individuals are motivated to flee. Of course, this is an overly broad generalization, but it still factors into the evaluation of bond in every case in Oklahoma.

Any experienced criminal defense attorney can work with you and your family to present a powerful argument that you are not a flight risk and that you will return to court to face your charges. Some of the tools we use to address the Court's concern about the risk of flight, include the following:

- Ties to the community: when someone has family and other substantial connections to the community, it is a factor that supports the defendant remaining in the jurisdiction.
- Lack of ties outside the community: conversely, if you do not have substantial ties out of state, it reduces the likelihood that you will have assistance in fleeing.

- Bond Conditions: the Court has wide discretion in setting bond with conditions on release. The right combination of bond conditions can give the Court confidence that you will return to Court.

- History on Bond: your appearance in court for previous charges can be an indicator that you will appear on your new case. Additionally, your defense attorney can argue a lack of failing to appear for court, if you have never been in trouble before, as you have never missed a court date!

Cash Bond

As previously stated, you can post the full amount of your bond to the Court or sheriff directly and be released on a cash bond. It is important you keep copies of the receipt if you post a cash bond, as the bond will be returned or exonerated at the conclusion of the case, whether convicted or not. The majority of criminal cases are resolved in three to six months, with exceptions, which means the money you gave to the court or jail will be returned in that same time frame.

Alternatively, you may seek a loan from a financial institution with collateral to get the cash for bond, which would save you the bondsman fee; however, a loan will take more time than a bonding company and comes with other costs, such as interests.

Surety Bond

The majority of those facing criminal charges hire a bail bondman, as the full amount of bond on many cases is too much to post in cash. Typically, a bail bondsman requires you to pay them ten percent (10%) of the total bail prior to the bondsman going through the process described in the previous paragraph (posting your bail at the jail or courthouse).

When you work with a bail bondsman, they guarantee you or your loved one's appearance at all future court appearances. If you or your loved one fail to appear at court, the bail bondsman will be liable for the total amount of bail, and they may seek to recover the total amount from you or seek to return you to court.

The bail bondsman will keep the percentage of bail you pay them at the conclusion of the case, regardless of the result, as opposed to the total amount being returned to you by the court/jail, if you post the bond. Ask around, check with the Better Business Bureau, and look at online reviews to determine the reliability of the bonding company or ask your attorney for a list of reputable bail bondsmen.

Conditional Bond

The bond conditions described above are another option for the court. When the court grants Conditional Bond without a surety or property, it is a true conditional bond. The term Conditional Bond means you do not have to pay cash to the court, or a bail bondman, and you are released pending court, so long as you comply with your bond conditions. Your Conditional Bond is based upon abiding by or performing a number of conditions, while out of custody.

Own Recognizance Bond

Additionally, in some Oklahoma counties or circumstances, individuals are released for non-violent offenses on their own recognizance, an O.R. Bond, which does not require any money being posted or conditions performed prior to release. An O.R. Bond, if granted, is the best option for you and your family, as it will allow you to return to work and use your funds for other necessary purposes, such as hiring the best criminal defense attorney.

Regardless of how you or your loved one gets out of jail during the case, it is an invaluable for your defense that you are out of custody. As discussed in a later chapter, you can do much good for your case and your attorney out of jail.

ARRAIGNMENT IN YOUR CASE

"Being a new client of John Cannon & Associates and having very little knowledge of how the justice and court system works, John was very helpful in easing my mind from day one at our first meeting in his office. He explained how it works, what would take place and did everything he said he would do. Court day he took charge and helped my wife that was terrified and helped her thru the whole process and everything went well. Thanks John!"

Richard

Regardless of the jurisdiction, you will appear before a judge or hearing officer shortly after being arrested for arraignment. In the military this is typically referred to as the "first reading", when your commander advises you of the charges and specification. In state and federal court, it is simply called an arraignment.

The Arraignment is the first time you will appear before the Court with jurisdiction to answer for the filed criminal charges brought against you. It is an important date concerning bail and when you learn your specific charges. At arraignment, you will stand before the judge, hopefully with your criminal defense attorney, and you will be informed of the charges filed against you by the prosecuting office, and be asked to enter a plea to the charges.

We previously discussed proposed charges by the arresting officer or law enforcement agency. The opinion of the arresting agency, their reports, and other information factors into the charges filed by the prosecuting office and, although the prosecutor must rely on competent evidence in deciding what charges to file, he/she has wide discretion on what offenses to file or allege against you. Prosecutorial discretion is sometimes misused, which an experienced criminal defense attorney can identify and begin fighting for you.

As discussed in a previous chapter, the arraignment date you received in custody may be incorrect. You need to hire an attorney or check on a regular basis with the judge handling the arraignment to ensure you appear at the right time, place, and date. Failing to appear for your arraignment can result in your bond/bail being revoked and potentially being denied. You will not be able to get out of jail without the assistance of an experienced criminal defense attorney if you are arrested for failing to appear in Court.

In Oklahoma state court proceedings, the document used to charge you is called the Information. The Information lists much of what your criminal defense attorney will need to begin defending your case. The Information filed in your Oklahoma state court criminal case will include the following:

- The Prosecutorial District and County where the charge is pending;
- Any and all defendants or co-defendants in your case;
- The name of each criminal offense alleged;
- Statutory reference for each charge, meaning the statutory authority for the alleged criminal offense;
- A brief factual summary of each charge, including: the date, the alleged victims, and what you are accused of doing; and
- The name and signature of an Assistant District Attorney filing the charge. In some counties, the prosecutor who files the charge will try the case; however, in other larger counties the prosecutor that filed the case may not ever be involved again.

How to Plea at Arraignment

The default plea at arraignment is Not Guilty. It is a non-confrontational appearance, and even if you and your attorney will seek a plea agreement from the beginning of your case, you should enter a plea of Not Guilty at arraignment. The prosecutor assigned to your case will likely not attend your arraignment; in fact, the other side may not ever be in the courtroom. The prosecutor has the burden of proving your guilty beyond a reasonable doubt. You want them to believe you will hold then to their burden before you receive a plea agreement that you are interested in accepting.

In Custody Arraignment

During In-custody arraignment, or an arraignment from jail, you will typically appear before the judge by video. The judge will provide you the same information indicated above; however, the time frame for arraignment for those in custody is much shorter than out of custody defendants. If charges are filed against you and you were never arrested a warrant will be issued for your arrest.

Although it may sound crazy, you can avoid being arrested all together after charges are filed, by hiring a bail bondsman to conduct a walk-through with you at jail. When you conduct a walk-through, you will not be taken into custody by law enforcement. Rather, you meet your bondsman at the jail and the process will take you a few hours or less. However long your walk-through takes, you will get to walk out of the jail the same day with your bail bondsman.

Information Presented at Arraignment

Arraignment is the first official date you face the charges filed against you, and in additional to the information previously discussed, the judge will advise you of your Constitutional Rights at arraignment: right to a jury trial, presumption of innocence, and the burden of proof, among other rights. You should discuss each of these rights at greater length with your criminal defense attorney. If your case is a felony, you and your criminal defense attorney will be advised of the assigned District Judge.

Who is Present at Arraignment?

Not all the parties that play a role in your criminal case will appear at arraignment. The judge that conducts the hearing is often not involved in your case beyond arraignment. The prosecutor in your case will likely not be present. Often, the prosecutor handling your case will not even get your file until after you are arraigned. Arraignments are typically attended by the judge, their staff, criminal defense attorneys, and all defendants with arraignment scheduled for the same day.

Regardless of whether or not the prosecutor in your case appears for arraignment, it is important that you keep your mouth shut and only answer the questions asked by the Court. The best way to avoid saying something about your case or otherwise that you cannot take back, is by hiring an experienced criminal defense attorney and allowing them to speak on your behalf at your arraignment.

In conclusion, arraignment is the first substantive step in your criminal defense case and concludes the beginning phase of your case. Once your criminal defense attorney identifies the prosecutor handing your case, he or she will be able to begin working towards the best possible outcome for you. The next section will cover the Criminal Defense in State Court.

SECTION THREE: CRIMINAL DEFENSE IN STATE COURT

STATE CRIMINAL DEFENSE

"An issue came about from my son's past recently and he was going to be charged with a felony and possibly do jail time. He had just got hired for a very good job that he could actually build a career out of. We were so worried about these felony charges, did some research, read some google reviews and found John Cannon to be the best attorney to help us. We made the call, gave them all the info that was brought forth to us about the charges, paid our retainer fee and he set up a case. The staff at Cannon & Associates were very courteous and professional. Anytime I had questions they would find answers in a timely manner and reassure me they had the case taken of. The day court arrived, John did his job and did it well! He got my son's felony charged reduced to misdemeanor and got the deferred sentencing reduced! He's the

man!! Now my son can finally move forward with his life and career!! Thank you, Cannon & Associates!"

Joanna

YOUR FIRST COURT DATE AND BEYOND

Time is critical, and you should act fast when you are facing criminal charges. Your first court date, your arraignment as discussed in a previous chapter, may be within a week of your arrest, which is not a lot of time to find and hire the right criminal defense attorney.

After arraignment, your case will be scheduled for a disposition date, on misdemeanor cases, or a preliminary hearing conference in a felony. The prosecutor handling your case will appear at the first court date and will be ready to discuss fighting your case or resolution. Therefore, it is important you appear with an experienced defense attorney, prepared to discuss your case.

Every court appearance in your case will be much smoother with an experienced criminal defense attorney. In many counties when you hire an attorney before court, your attorney will be able to appear on your behalf, meaning you will not have to go to court, or you will have your case heard at the beginning of the docket, which will allow you to leave the courthouse quickly.

How Often Should I Meet with My Defense Attorney?

How often you should meet with your criminal defense attorney will depend on a number of factors in your case. Although you may want to meet with or receive updates from your criminal defense attorney on a regular basis, the frequency that you should meet with your defense team is determined by the status of your case. After you retain your defense team, they will seek to obtain

Informed Criminal Defense

discovery in your case as well as communicate with the prosecutor to find out their position in your case.

The time it takes for your attorney to obtain information often takes longer than either of you would like to wait. In some cases, things move very quickly, and you will receive information and have phone/email exchanges from your attorney on a very rapid basis. In other cases, you and your attorney must wait from fifteen (15) to forty-five (45) days for useful information from the prosecutor.

The seriousness, complexity, and amount of charges you and your criminal defense attorney are facing plays a major role in the length of time you must wait for answers.

Our criminal defense team at Cannon & Associates requests police reports directly from the law enforcement agency which is or has conducted the investigation into your case. However, the information provided directly to your attorney is limited. We will not learn everything we want to know about your case or the investigation through law enforcement or an open records request. We will need to meet with the prosecutor on your case in order to obtain all the evidence available.

The earlier your criminal defense attorney is able to meet with the prosecutor to discuss your case the better. The earlier the more likely the prosecutor on your case has not reached a decision on how they feel about your case, which is a great opportunity for your counsel to impact how the prosecutor sees you!

It is important when interviewing criminal defense attorneys to get an idea of how long they think it will take to have real answers about the process in your case. You are entitled to know at the very least the following: what attorney will be personally handling your case, who can you speak to in the firm, what is the timeline going forward, and what are reasonable expectations at each point of your case.

Should I speak with Law Enforcement without an Attorney?

Law enforcement is not legally obligated to tell you the truth. In very limited circumstances, your attorney can use law enforcement lying to you against the prosecution's case; however, it generally will not help you. However, if you lie to police it can negatively impact you!

You cannot make a mistake when talking to police. The safest bet; do not speak to police, hire a criminal defense attorney that knows their business. Then and only then should you consider the option of telling your story to law enforcement. An experienced criminal defense attorney cannot change the facts; however, your defense attorney can advise you whether or not you should tell your version of events to the investigator or simply force the prosecution to attempt to meet their burden, beyond a reasonable doubt, at trial.

A dedicated criminal defense attorney will reach out to interested law enforcement and advise them that you are represented by counsel and should not be contacted except through your attorney's office. My firm requests investigators, police, and law enforcement direct all questions and requests of our clients to my office and in writing. An experienced criminal defense attorney can act as a protective barrier from missteps with police, such as unintended confessions, and police contact before you are prepared to tell your story.

Generally, without an experienced criminal defense attorney you will not be able to forecast law enforcement's actions or investigation. However, with our office you may get a preview of law enforcement's intention or the course of their investigation prior to or' without appearing for an in-person, possibly highly damaging interrogation.

What Can a Defense Attorney Do Before Charges Are Filed?

As discussed in the previous chapter, an experienced and dedicated criminal defense attorney will notify the law enforcement agency investigating your case that you are represented by counsel,

Informed Criminal Defense

should not be contacted directly, and that requests should be submitted through your attorney's office. Although prosecutors and police are not obligated to comply with your attorney's request, if your attorney has earned a reputation of respect he/she may be able to find out the contemplated charges and other useful information for your defense.

Your defense attorney, as your advocate, can begin to tell your story to law enforcement and/or the prosecutor, without you making a statement. This information could prove your innocence, which would stop charges from ever being filed, and save you and your family substantial time and stress. Your attorney can provide information to convince the prosecutor to file or law enforcement to present less serious charges. Your attorney can cast doubt on the credibility of witnesses, or provide contact information for witnesses beneficial to your case that should be interviewed before a decision to charge you with a crime has been made by the prosecutor.

Finally, the right criminal defense attorney can investigate your case before favorable statements are forgotten by witnesses, or erased from their memory due to substantial contact with investigators building a case against you. Although witnesses are not obligated to speak to criminal defense investigators, it is always a useful process to pursue. I have seen cases won or greatly improved for my clients by the information discovered or exposed by the dedicated investigators I have worked with over the years.

You need a Fierce Advocate®. Your case and your future depend on hiring the right attorney for the job. **We're proud of the fact we have more 5-Star Google Reviews than 99% of attorneys in Oklahoma**; however, that alone does not mean we are the right defense team for you. Do your homework, interview attorneys, and prepare to fight your case.

STATE COURT CRIMINAL PROCEEDINGS OVERVIEW

"They are hard-working, professional, and reliable. They will work hard for you no matter your circumstances and get the best results possible for you."

Samantha

No two criminal cases are the same. You may ask what factors cause the process to vary from case to case: specific procedures for the county in which your case is pending; the docket and judge assigned to your case; the prosecutor handing your case; and the volume of cases on the docket.

Although every Oklahoma state court criminal proceeding has elements that are unique, there are general aspects of the Oklahoma state court criminal process that do not change. Now to the overview.

1ST STEP - CRIMINAL ARREST

Most criminal cases begin with someone being arrested under suspicion of a criminal offense. The fear of losing one's freedom and the unknown of being arrested is a dangerous motivator to speak to police. Exercise your right to remain silent and wait to meet with your chosen criminal defense attorney.

2ND STEP – BOOKING IN JAIL

After you are arrested, you will be booked into jail. This is another moment that people may make a poor decision and implicate themselves in the case. Prior to bonding out of jail, a bond will be set based on the presumed charges presented by the arresting agency. Most jails use a predetermined bond "schedule that includes every crime in the book to set your" initial bond.

Next you will go through in-processing, which may take over 12 hours. During this time, you should be allowed to make a phone call, and will be assigned a cell in the jail. It is crucial you contact someone who can assist you in retaining criminal defense counsel and a bondsman, if you have the funds for both. **Do not say anything about your case to anyone, especially on the phone from jail, as these calls are recorded and can be used against you in court.**

3RD STEP – INVESTIGATION

The law enforcement officer or officers involved in your arrest will draft a citation or police reports, which are given to the prosecutor to review and determine what if any charges will be filed in your circumstance. In simple cases, the investigation by law enforcement will typically be limited to the interaction between you and police at the time of your arrest. However, more complex matters may include detectives, interviews, and more substantial investigation.

4TH STEP – CHARGES FILED

Once the prosecutor has all the information necessary to make a filing decision, the prosecutor will review the reports or investigation, sometimes with police, and decide on filing criminal charges or not against you. Prosecutors are held to a lower burden in filing charges than at trial. Therefore, many criminal cases are filed that the government cannot prove at trial.

An experienced criminal defense attorney can research the charges brought against you and potentially convince the prosecutor, the judge, or a jury that the prosecutor cannot make a case against you beyond a reasonable doubt. Evaluating the strength of the government's evidence to support their case against you is vital to your criminal defense.

5TH STEP - ARRAIGNMENT

Once the prosecutor makes a filing decision in your case, an Information is filed in District Court, and you will appear at Arraignment. During the arraignment, you will be notified of your charges and your case will be set for another court date. In the interim, your criminal defense attorney can seek to meet with the prosecutor on your case and fight for you.

6TH STEP - EVALUATING YOUR CASE

After charges are filed, your criminal defense attorney should receive the government's evidence, or discovery, in your case, including some or all of the following: police reports, photographs, audio recordings, and video evidence. An experienced criminal defense attorney can evaluate the government's evidence to give you a good idea of the likelihood of success, if you fight your case or seek to suppress evidence in your case.

Once you and your criminal defense attorney have a good sense of the government's case, you can discuss options and likelihood for success with fighting your case or seeking an agreed resolution. This is one of the most important aspects of criminal defense, in that it is crucial you work with an attorney that will clearly explain the complex issues involved with these important decisions.

In felony cases in Oklahoma, you will proceed to Preliminary Hearing Conference after arraignment. Your attorney and the prosecutor will discuss your charges and begin communication about moving forward on your case.

7TH STEP - NEGOTIATIONS

After evaluating your case, if you and your criminal defense attorney decide that you want to resolve your case without fighting or having a trial, then it is time to seek an agreement with the prosecutor.

Our team will work with you closely to help develop a compelling narrative for why you should be given leniency based on the mitigation or extenuation in your case, ie what about you or the circumstance warrants your avoiding prison or a conviction.

Storytelling is an important part of any case; however, working with a criminal defense attorney that can expertly tell your story is invaluable. When your criminal defense attorney builds a compelling story about your life and circumstances, it may give the judge or prosecutor reason to grant leniency that you may not have received otherwise.

8TH STEP - LITIGATION

You have a Constitutional right to make the government prove its case against you beyond a reasonable doubt. Although not all cases warrant exercising this right, it is important to work with a criminal defense attorney that is confident in their ability to fight for you, including taking your case to jury trial, if you are innocent or over-charged by the government. Your criminal defense team's ability to investigating your case and tell a powerful story of your innocence at trial or fight for you in motion practice is key to success in litigating your case.

In felony cases in Oklahoma, you have the right to a preliminary hearing pursuant to Oklahoma Statute Title 22 Section 258. The prosecutor has the burden of proof at the preliminary hearing; however, the burden is much lower than at trial. The rules of evidence apply, but your attorney may strike harsh blows to the prosecution's case, if prepared.

It is key to work with an experienced attorney at every phase of your case, especially jury trial. The presentation of your case at trial is more show than law, which requires a great storyteller and a compelling tale for your innocence.

Again, jury trial is a show. Once the jury is selected, the substantive trial begins with opening statements. The prosecution has the burden to prove your guilt beyond a reasonable doubt, and the jury must be unanimous. Your attorney is allowed to question every witness and piece of evidence presented by the prosecution. Your attorney will present your case to the jury, and should fight for your innocence by attacking weaknesses in the prosecution's case, and by telling your story. Jury instructions or the law provided to the jury can be argued on your behalf.

Once the instructions are set, closing arguments are made and the jury deliberates. The jury will return a verdict. Upon a not guilty verdict, you will be released from any further proceedings. Upon a guilty verdict, your case will be set over for sentencing and you will remain in custody or be placed in custody, unless the judge grants your attorney's request for release pending sentencing.

There are many tools available to the criminal defense attorney to fight for clients at every level of our criminal justice system. It is important that you work with a criminal defense attorney capable of assisting you in exercising your rights if you want to fight your case.

9TH STEP - RESOLUTION

Whether you take your case to trial or reach a resolution or plea agreement, all criminal cases must come to an end at some point. When you fight your case, it will either result in a dismissal of charges or you may be found guilty at trial. However, if you are found guilty, you will be sentenced in your case. You and your criminal defense attorney will likely appear at more than one court appearance in the process of seeking the best possible outcome on your case.

In a felony case, you and your attorney will appear before the District Judge that will conduct the jury trial in your case, if you decide to take that route. Additionally, your criminal defense attorney will continue working on the prosecutor of your case. You now have the options of reaching a plea agreement, fighting your case, or entering a blind plea and arguing the sentence of your case to the District Judge.

When you resolve your case by plea agreement or participation in a program, there is certainty to what the future of your case holds. You should never enter a plea in your criminal case, unless you have discussed your case and options with your criminal defense attorney, and you are confident you have explored available defenses and resolutions without a plea. However, if you have evaluated all options and want to move forward with a plea or entering a program, it is important that your attorney explains all your options and what those options mean going forward.

10TH STEP - BEYOND RESOLUTION

You can seek an immediate expungement, if you win your case (in most instances), either at trial or by Court order to have the record sealed. However, if you are found guilty at trial or reach a resolution on your case, you will be sentenced. Typically, if you are found guilty at trial, you will face jail or prison time. You are entitled to appeal your sentence after trial if you are convicted. It is important to work with an experienced appellate attorney if you decide to take this course of action.

When you resolve your case by plea agreement or participation in a program, you will have conditions and terms you must complete, in order to be successful on probation. Probation is an opportunity to resolve your case, minimize the exposure you would have, if you proceeded to trial, and have certainty about what is required of you.

The terms of probation can vary greatly, which is why it is important to hire an experienced criminal defense attorney to assist you in minimizing the costs and difficulty of your probation and to help ensure you understand exactly what is required of you and by when.

CONCLUSION TO STATE COURT PROCEEDINGS

Although this summary of proceedings is brief, it touches upon all the steps in most state court criminal defense cases. This process is specific to state court criminal proceedings; however, the majority of this process is applicable to federal criminal practice, misdemeanors, or city charges. In all criminal defense cases, whether you want to enter a plea or fight your case, it is important that you seek to tell a compelling story. When you work with an experienced criminal defense attorney, your likelihood of obtaining the best possible outcome increases greatly.

You are entitled to fight your criminal case at every step of the process, including taking your case to jury trial where the government must prove your guilt beyond a reasonable doubt or you will be found not guilty and your case will be dismissed.

Reading one section of a book by an experienced Oklahoma criminal defense attorney cannot prepare you for making some of the most important decisions in your life. We are Fierce Advocates® for every client we serve and hope to have the opportunity to serve you and your family, in part by simplifying the process and helping you make the best decisions at every step of state court criminal proceedings.

THE POWER OF ACCUSATIONS

"I've had a great experience working with Cannon & Associates. With regards to my particular case, the team was diligent, trustworthy, extremely knowledgeable, and compassionate. He truly went above and beyond then ultimately secured the best outcome for me. I highly recommend Cannon & Associates to anyone looking for an attorney in Oklahoma City area."

PJ

The power of accusations in our criminal justice system cannot be overstated. False identification and false allegations are far more prevalent that you would believe. It is the duty of dedicated investigators and criminal defense attorneys to ensure those that have been falsely accused receive a great defense, and that their story is told.

It does not take much in order to be charged with a crime. In fact, it only takes an <u>ALLEGATION</u>.

The decision on how to approach a criminal accusation, especially one resulting in a felony charge, is very important. You have the right to competent criminal defense counsel; use it. Hiring the right Oklahoma criminal defense attorney with the experience necessary to assist you through these difficult decisions will be an invaluable investment. An experienced defense attorney will help you identify the best course of action and defenses that you should explore, including investigating your narrative, to build a strong defense.

In many cases of false accusations, if your defense attorney is able to present a compelling narrative of your innocence, including witness statements, to the prosecutor, your charges may be dismissed before trial, or you may never be charged. You need a Fierce Advocate® to protect your rights, your liberty, and your freedom, if you are facing false accusations.

It is scary to think one individual's misrepresentation, mistake, or even lie, concerning your involvement in a criminal act can result in your being prosecuted; however, it is true. This flaw of our system plays a central role in why many attorneys are called to defend the criminal accused. No attorney can guarantee an outcome to you or your family. However, we guarantee that we will fight for you and use every tool available to us, if you are falsely accused.

Accusations and Negotiation

Defendants justly accused are on the opposite end of the spectrum from those that are falsely accused. They need just as good a defense as those that are falsely accused; in fact, sometimes they need better representation. Our clients that acknowledge some form of wrongdoing often desire to resolve their case by negotiating an agreement with the prosecutor.

Whether you want to fight your case to the end or you know you want to seek a plea agreement, it is important that you have a good understanding of all your options. The following are takeaways about plea negotiations from over a decade of being a defense attorney and prosecutor.

The first key takeaway in plea negotiations is to understand; all parties have motivations to resolve your case without trial. Stated another way, the prosecutor is motivated to resolve your case with a plea.

The prosecutor is not able to try each of the cases on his or her docket, which is continually having cases added to it. Judicial economy and the sheer amount of time it takes to litigate each case requires prosecutors make an offer to resolve the case. Otherwise, each courthouse would come to a grinding halt, as it is impossible for the majority of cases to be litigated. The prosecutor's motivations are different that your motivations; however, that does not make them any less real.

The next takeaway, the prosecution is not obligated to make an offer to you. Most prosecution offices have a policy that plea offers must be made by a certain court date; however, the law does not require prosecutors offer to resolve your case.

In my experience, over 99% of criminal defendants receive some version of a plea agreement over the course of the case. However, that offer can come at any time and can take many forms. It is important that you work with a criminal defense attorney that understands the chess match of plea negotiations in order to achieve the best offer possible.

The next important consideration is the fact that the best plea offers come from an analysis of multiple factors. Most prosecutors do not know everything about you and your situation, unless your defense attorney is able to tell a compelling story about you, supported with documentation.

KEY FACTORS IN PLEA NEGOTIATIONS

"Intelligent. Helpful. Fierce. Ready. Loved. I CAN'T tell you how much they have helped me through my case, from start the finish they were there for me."

Jacqui

Some prosecutors are more receptive than others to consider the information your criminal defense attorney can bring to them. However, they all need a better picture of the situations than police reports provide. The following are factors that have a major impact on what the best plea recommendation may be in your case:

- The seriousness of your charge(s);
- The number of charges or cases pending against you;
- Your criminal background, if any;
- The impact of the case on any victim(s);
- The victim(s) history with the system;
- Strength of the prosecution's case;
- Strength of your factual defense;
- Suppression or legal problems with the prosecution's case;
- Politics and policies of the prosecuting office;
- Quality of the defense case your attorney can build;
- The experience of your criminal defense attorney; and
- The reputation of your criminal defense attorney

Seriousness of your Charges

It goes without saying that a misdemeanor DUI will subject you to a lesser range of punishment than drug trafficking. However, what must be said, is that there is a reason (good, bad, or ugly) that impacted you getting into the situation that resulted in your criminal case. Stated another way, the influences and events of your life that led to your being charged are powerful, and the prosecutor has no idea what they are, unless your defense attorney can show them.

Yes, you will potentially face a number of years in prison for any serious felony charge. However, when your defense attorney builds a compelling story of who you are and how you got to the place that lead to your charges, it paints a powerful picture for the prosecutor to consider in reaching a just resolution in your case.

This process starts from the beginning of your case with identifying witnesses, potential mental/emotional evaluations, and any available information that can document the impacts in your life. Your journey is not an excuse for conduct, but it does provide a bigger picture for the prosecutor to evaluate, which can greatly impact the outcome of a negotiated plea in your case.

Factual Defenses

Prosecutors do not like to lose, and they use their negotiation authority to resolve a number of cases they fear losing at trial. Most prosecutors try to negotiate a plea on any case they fear they will lose at trial. Prosecutors rely on experienced criminal defense attorneys to explain a client's defense, in order to get a better picture of the weakness of their case. In some instances, if your defense attorney can show the prosecutor a compelling enough argument, your case may be dismissed outright.

Experienced criminal defense attorneys use investigators to identify witnesses and capture testimony and evidence that will support the defense. Law enforcement stops most investigations as soon as someone is arrested, which leaves a substantial part of the story to be uncovered by your defense team.

When your defense team is able to present a compelling story of your innocence or exhibit problems in the government's case, it will likely result in a far better plea offer from the prosecutor. Whomever you hire as your counsel, ensure they know your story and can present it powerfully to the prosecutor at the appropriate time.

Legal Defenses

Law enforcement must have authority to search your person and your property, a legal maxim that can result in evidence being excluded from your case in many circumstances. When your defense attorney identifies a strong argument for the exclusion of evidence or police misconduct in your case, it will result in the prosecutor making you a better offer.

Returning to the maxim that prosecutors do not like to lose, experienced prosecutors will take action to avoid their case being dismissed by the Court on a legal issue. Whether your attorney files a motion and a hearing is held or they simply identify the issue to the prosecutor, identification of a legal issue will cause the prosecutor to re-evaluate the case and often it will result in a more favorable offer being made. Whether the prosecutor improves the offer in your case or not after a legal problem is identified, your attorney can use the issue to fight your case or argue the same to the Court.

Your Criminal History

Many people have a past and although your past will follow you in the criminal justice system, it does not have to define you. Prosecutors do start their evaluation of a plea recommendation in your case by looking at your criminal history. However, if the process stopped there, then there would be little use for an experienced criminal defense attorney to fight for you. I have represented hundreds of people that have returned to the justice system after being imprisoned, and many of them were able to participate in a program or treatment option in lieu of simply returning to prison. But that always came after we worked together to build a plan for the client's future.

Unfortunately, many criminal defendants did not have a Fierce Advocate® on a previous journey through the criminal justice system and were put in a place of taking a less than great plea offer or going to trial. We cannot guarantee a client will avoid prison; however, we do guarantee finding your story and building a plan to do everything possible to keep you out of prison, and hopefully avoid a conviction.

When an experienced prosecutor learns a compelling client story from an experienced criminal defense attorney, the past of that client often matters far less than where the person is now. I repeat, your past does not have to define you. When you fight for your future, you may be surprised at the outcome you can achieve despite your past.

Victim Information

First off, crimes that do not involve an individual victim are easier to obtain the best outcome. Crimes that victimize entities or the state are still prosecuted; however, the prosecutor does not have to explain to an individual an outcome on the case. "Victimless crimes" remove one part of the equation, which makes it easier for your defense attorney to focus on your interests in negotiations.

In cases with individual victims, the process of seeking the best outcome is more complicated than "victim-less" cases. However, the credibility of every witness, including victims/complaining witnesses, matter in criminal cases. Prosecutors are responsible for evaluating the strength of their case, which includes the witness testimony that your case is based upon. Many factors impact the credibility of the victim in your case, including motivation to lie, history of truthfulness, bias against you, and how many versions of the events the witness has told. It is the responsibility of your criminal defense attorney to point out the credibility issues with the victim in your case; to the jury, if you go to trial or to the prosecutor, if you are seeking an agreed resolution in your case.

You should not contact the victim in your case directly; however, your defense attorney is entitled to speak to every witness in the case. When your defense attorney has the opportunity to meet with or speak with the victim, it can sometimes impact their position on what outcome they want in the case, which may help your defense attorney seek a better outcome for you.

The Prosecutor's Role

Prosecutors are uniquely tasked with representing or advocating the interests of multiple parties, chiefly any victims involved and the community at large. Prosecution office politics and policies have a major impact in the approach the specific attorney prosecuting your case will take as well. Some offices take a hardline of prison-time-only offers on certain offenses, which the assigned prosecutor on your case cannot overrule. Even in offices that do not have hard-line rules on plea offers or outcomes of cases, your opposition is responsible to consider more parties than you and your defense attorney.

When your criminal defense attorney knows the prosecutor in your case or can research their background and develop an understanding of the prosecutor's mindset, the chance of a great outcome on your case increases. In the end, prosecutors are people, and each individual prosecutor has different triggers or issues that can make them feel compassion for you, or the opposite.

When your freedom is on the line, you want to ensure the defense attorney you hire can identify what the prosecutor on your case truly cases about and speak to those issues/pain points in your case. You will be amazed at the difference it can make in some cases, if your attorney can speak directly to the concerns of the prosecutor in your case.

Mitigation and Extenuation

Two broad factors not previously covered that impact plea negotiations in your case are mitigating and extenuating circumstances. When this type of information is accepted by the prosecutor or judge, it may lessen the charges or penalty you face.

- **Mitigating circumstances** lessen the moral or legal consequences of a crime. An example of mitigation in your case may include you acted out of necessity to provide for your family or you.
- **Extenuating circumstances** excuse or justify conduct.

Experience and Reputation of your Criminal Defense Team

You would not put your life in the hands of an inexperienced doctor, you should be just as careful with the defense attorney you hire to protect your future and your freedom. Prosecutors know which defense attorneys can fight and are willing to take a case to trial and which attorneys will eventually give up.

Prosecutors talk about defense attorneys all the time and know which criminal defense attorneys must be taken seriously and which are not willing to fight for their clients. Your chosen criminal defense attorney has a reputation, either good or bad, and right or wrong, it will impact the outcome of your case. It is in your interest to hire a great criminal defense attorney that you like and that your trust with your future.

RESOLUTION OPTIONS IN CRIMINAL CASES

"John is one impressive attorney who is super knowledgeable, quick witted, confident, passionate and a true advocate for all clients. He has a heart for military clients and helped me get involved in the Veteran Diversion Group. He gave me the best advice and you can not go wrong with this group. Literally, once my case finally got charged, the case was closed within 2 months. Yes, I said CLOSED (charges dismissed) The credit is truly due to John Cannon & Tom Stone's knowledge. Thank you so very much to everyone involved in handling my case. Also a special shout out to Brittany who helped with my case."

Andrew

There are a variety of potential outcomes in a criminal case; however, your options will be unique from any other case. Having your case dismissed is obviously the best outcome in a criminal case. Your case can be dismissed as a result of your attorney convincing the prosecutor that it should be dismissed, by winning a suppression issue, or a not guilty verdict at trial. I have had many clients with each outcome, and they are all wonderful, because it is the best possible result for your client. However, most cases are not dismissed, which leads to the other outcomes of a criminal case.

Other than dismissal of your charges, a deferred sentence is the best realistic outcome. A deferred sentence means the judgment or conviction is deferred, or set off, for a number of months or years. During the delay, you will be required to complete a number of probation requirements; your attorney can and should work to make the conditions of probation as easy as possible. Upon successfully completing probation, and staying out of trouble, the case will be dismissed on the date the case was deferred.

Stated another way, if you receive a two-year deferred, the sentencing date is scheduled for two years from the date of your plea. On your sentencing date, if you have completed the terms of probation and stayed out of trouble, the case will be dismissed. Deferred sentences are delayed gratification; if you can stay the course and complete probation, your case will be dismissed eventually, which is the best outcome possible.

Once your defense attorney is able to secure a deferred sentence, the next step is to seek the shortest deferred sentence possible, with achievable probation expectations being placed upon you.

In more serious cases, or if you have a criminal record, you may not be able to have sentencing set off for a number of years, i.e., receive a deferred sentence. In those circumstances the next best thing is to avoid imposition of your sentence, or avoid jail/prison time. This resolution is called a suspended sentence. It is unfortunately a conviction; however, the period of incarceration (part of any conviction) is suspended or set off based on conditions.

In a suspended sentence, you receive a felony or misdemeanor conviction; however, incarceration is set off, similar to the deferred sentence that delays a conviction. When you successfully complete a suspended sentence, you will no longer be at risk of being incarcerated; however, you will still have a conviction.

Like the deferred sentence, the terms of your probation on a suspended sentence either increases or decreases your likelihood for success on probation. For most criminal charges, you may now seek expungement, sealing, of your criminal record even after a conviction once enough time has passed.

The next worse outcome in a criminal case is suspended-in-part. The suspended-in-part sentence includes a period of incarceration and a period of suspended incarceration (probation). The make-up or ratio of both can vary greatly, and although no one wants to receive a period of incarceration, a partial period of incarceration is far better than a lengthy prison sentence. In very serious cases, if we are unable to avoid prison time for our client, we will seek a suspended-in-part sentence to minimize their time away from family behind bars.

The most serious outcome in any criminal case is incarceration or prison. When all else fails in plea negotiations and you do not want to go to trial, you may be left with a plea agreement for a prison sentence. In some instances, a prison sentence is better than suspended-in-part, as you do not have exposure on the back end for the period of probation.

Your case and future depend on hiring an experienced criminal defense attorney to help you understand your options; decide the best course of action in your case; and fight to get you the best outcome possible.

State Court Probation

During probation, you must comply with the terms or rules of your probation, which were entered by the judge in court. On probation for a deferred sentence, your case will be dismissed, if you successfully complete probation, all the terms are satisfied, and you do not have a new criminal allegation. On probation for a suspended sentence, you will no longer be at risk of going to jail, but will have a conviction, if you successfully complete the requirements of probation. It is important to have an understanding of probation, as statistics indicate a high likelihood that you will have some form of probation, if your case is not dismissed.

In fact, over ninety-five percent of criminal cases in state courts are resolved without a trial and some form of probation follows. A skilled criminal defense attorney can help you fight for dismissal of charges; however, if that is unsuccessful, he or she will work to provide you the best possible resolution, so you may compare that option with going to trial on your case.

Whether you want to fight your case or not, skilled defense attorneys fight to obtain the best plea offer in your case from the prosecutor. When you have a favorable deal to consider, it gives you options in evaluating going to trial or accepting an agreed resolution. Even the most steadfast clients that are going to trial appreciate options to consider. There are unlimited options for what conditions of probation can be required in your case. However, when you and your defense attorney identify the services that will be best for you on probation, it is often possible to present a probation plan to the prosecutor that will be accepted.

Probation is an important part of the agreement or contract entered into by prosecutors and defendants. The parties must reach an agreement on the specific terms of probation, in order for a plea to be entered. Prosecutors appreciate when your defense attorney presents a plan, and it is best if you work with your counsel to prepare a proposal.

Prosecutors often have a default probation plan for cases, which they are often willing to modify, if your defense attorney can explain a better plan it may very well be accepted by the prosecutor. Once we identify a probation plan with our client, we task the client to begin completing the terms of the plan. Oftentimes, when prosecutors see that you have been proactive in completing terms of probation before entering your plea, the final terms of probation will be much easier to complete.

Obtaining substance abuse counseling, treatment, or even inpatient rehabilitation will not only be good for your health if you have a substance abuse issue, but it is also vital to improve how the prosecutor and judge perceive you. Clients with substance abuse charges will receive a better offer or plea bargain in their case by simply obtaining counseling or treatment.

Similarly, when you pay victims whole, such as paying restitution for property crimes or theft, prior to sentencing in your case, it will also greatly improve how the sentencing judge and prosecutor see you and your case.

Understand, you cannot directly provide restitution to the victim. You may however work with your attorney to present a proposal to the prosecutor to repay all or a portion of the requested restitution. All of these actions are steps towards making the victim whole or being proactive in your treatment needs in your case. The prosecutor or judge will consider your steps in making the victim whole prior to setting your sentence.

We work with each client to prepare a probation plan and exactly what will be required of them if they decide to enter a guilty plea. Storytelling is alive and well in criminal defense. Your ability to tell your story, with the guidance of an experienced criminal defense attorney, is vital to reaching the best possible outcome in your case. Creating a plan with your attorney and sticking to it is key in this arena.

Do I Simply Have to Stay Out of Trouble on Probation?

No, probation in some respects can be more difficult than a jail or prison sentence. Often, probation comes with multiple terms, costs, and expectations that must be met in order to not fail and receive jail time or worse. You can be sentenced to prison for the entire length of your suspended sentence for violating probation. You can be sentenced to prison for the maximum sentence on your charge for violating probation on a deferred sentence. This is not said to scare you, rather it is to say, you have much to do to be successful after entering probation in your case.

Unfortunately, hundreds of defendants every year enter into plea agreements they know they will be unable to complete or fail to abide by the terms of probation and end up right back in the system. The importance of understanding every expectation of you on probation cannot be overstated. You should ensure you make early and often contact with your probation officer to ensure you are both on the same page concerning your requirements.

Plus, you **must review the terms of probation ordered by the Court and make sure you follow those terms.** It is not a defense to a probation violation to say, "my probation officer told me I had done everything required." You entered into a contract (plea agreement) with the prosecutor, you must ensure you are complying with that agreement.

Often probation violations are technical, i.e. not criminal acts. Life happens, and sometimes things get rough; however, that is not a sufficient excuse for violating a term of your probation, or failing to attend a class or complete community service. This is just one of the reasons why we fight so hard to get the best terms of probation for every client, and encourage them to complete the terms they can before we resolve their case.

Often, criminal defendants are so happy to have their case behind them they forget the importance of staying on top of their probation, which is why my firm goes over the terms of probation with every client before the day we resolve the client's case; the day of the plea; and after sentencing. Additionally, we encourage clients to meet with their probation officer early and often to ensure both are on the same page.

What Happens after a Probation Violation?

The terms of your probation are your part of an agreement or contract with the prosecution (the state). In exchange for not going to jail (suspended sentence) or avoiding a conviction (deferred sentence); you are required to complete all the terms of your probation and avoid new criminal charges. When you are successful with the terms of your probation, then you will receive the expected outcome when you finish probation. Conversely, if the prosecutor believes you have violated probation, then you will face an application in court that may take away the terms of your agreement.

In deferred sentence probation, if you have an alleged violation of probation, the prosecutor will file an Application to Accelerate, i.e. hold your sentencing immediately, with the potential of your receiving a conviction or jail time.

In suspended sentence probation, if you have an alleged violation of probation, the prosecutor will file an Application to Revoke, which can result in your probation being taken away and you serving jail or prison time instead of probation. It is important to have experienced criminal defense counsel if you are accused of violating a condition or multiple conditions of your probation.

No proceeding in state court affords a party more protections than a criminal defendant prior to a verdict or entry of a plea agreement. The government has the only burden, and it is beyond a reasonable doubt. After you enter a plea, you forfeit many of your rights, including a trial. The government still has the burden to prove you violated probation prior to the Court taking action against you; however, the process is more administrative than criminal, i.e. **did you or did you not violate the agreement for probation.**

The burden of proof is preponderance of the evidence. The process of an alleged probation violation is more administrative than judicial, as the determination as to whether you did or did not violate your probation is a technical determination. At hearing, the prosecutor need only present a limited amount of evidence to meet the low burden of proof that you violated probation, and your deferred sentence can turn into a conviction, or you can be sentenced to jail or prison. It is crucial you obtain experienced counsel, if faced with the harsh reality of contesting a probation violation, to assist you through your options and presenting all the defenses available to you.

There are multiple options to consider with an experienced attorney before exercising your right to a contested hearing before a judge, in which you do not know the outcome. You are entitled to a hearing before the judge on an Application to Accelerate or

Revoke; however, your defense attorney may be able to reach a resolution in your case without the exposure of a hearing.

CONSEQUENCES OF A CONVICTION

"John has all the qualities one would need in a lawyer. Smarts, compassion, advocacy skills, and experience. He genuinely cares about people and it shows through actions. I highly recommend John for anyone needing an attorney."

Jamaal

Being convicted of a felony is one of the most serious consequences one can face, especially with the collateral consequences that come from a felony conviction. The most well-known consequence of a felony conviction is obvious, incarceration, which can consist of a year or less time in a county jail, or up to life in prison.

Collateral consequences are the longest lasting punishment in most felony cases; the secondary effects not directly related to the sentence passed down or as part of a felony plea agreement. These consequences cause the denial of rights and privileges afforded to citizens without a felony conviction. Some of these consequences include loss of driving privileges, denial of a liquor store license, loss of the right to vote, loss of the right to possess a firearm, loss of the ability to serve in the Armed Services. The following career opportunities are all but lost after a felony conviction as well:

- Licensed Attorney
- Medical doctor, dentistry, chiropractor, veterinary medicine, nursing, pharmacology, psychology; and other medical careers
- Accountant

- Architect
- Counseling: Marriage; Mental Health; Family; and others;
- Licensed Realtor or real estate appraiser
- Law Enforcement: FBI, CIA, Highway Patrol, and Police
- Licensed Pawnbroker
- Bail Bondsman
- Court Reporter

This list is extensive, but not exhaustive of the rights, privileges, and opportunities forfeited upon becoming a convicted felon. This list is focused on the consequences of a felony conviction on rights and privileges under Oklahoma law; however, there are consequences under federal law, local ordinances, and administrative consequences which are not listed here.

A felony conviction may follow you and your family the rest of your life. When facing a felony, you have limited opportunities to avoid the long-lasting effects of a felony conviction: enter a plea agreement to avoid a felony offense, fight your case with the assistance of an experienced criminal defense attorney, or seek redress through an appeal. There is light at the end of many felony convictions, as recent changes to the law allow a person to expunge (seal) a felony conviction after the specified number of years has passed.

DIVERSION PROGRAMS IN OKLAHOMA

"John has all the qualities one would need in a lawyer. Smarts, compassion, advocacy skills, and experience. He genuinely cares about people and it shows through actions. I highly recommend John for anyone needing an attorney."
Antonio

The majority of offenders that find themselves in the criminal justice system have some form of trauma, substance dependency, or mental health that plays a role in their being in the system. Diversion Programs were created and have had much success in our criminal justice system as they are designed to help offenders that suffer from these issues. Diversion Programs are a more serious form of probation that mere supervision, but they are designed to provide an option for offenders, short of going to prison.

No one wants to participate in intensive probation; however, going to prison is even more worrisome. Fortunately, there are many resources and diversion options to consider before accepting the fate of a prison sentence. One of the greatest alternatives to prison is criminal diversion. The types and availability of these programs differ between courts; however, Diversion Programs are an important resource to consider, if you are facing the potential of prison time.

There are a number of diversion programs in state criminal courts across Oklahoma. Some of these programs are under the District Attorney's power of deferred prosecution. In deferred prosecution, the District Attorney dismisses your criminal case upon your acceptance into an applicable Diversion Program. Generally, you will sign a contract agreeing to participate in the program, which advises you if you are unsuccessful in the diversion program, your criminal case will be refiled, and you will be dismissed from the diversion program.

Veterans' Diversion programs are the most common deferred prosecution programs. The majority of Diversion Programs in Oklahoma however are not deferred prosecution agreements. Rather, they are "courts" or intensive probation, in which you enter a plea to your criminal charges prior to being admitted or accepted into the specific diversion program. When a criminal defendant enters the majority of diversion programs, a contract is signed that includes the benefit of participation in the program, including; your charges being dismissed upon successful completion; not serving jail or prison time, and; receiving/participating in treatment options.

In the unfortunate event a criminal defendant fails the Diversion Program, he or she will be sentenced based on the contract signed prior to entering the program, and may be sent to jail or even prison. Diversion programs are run by individual counties, which means each of the 77 counties in Oklahoma has their own procedure for application, admission, and successful completion of the programs. Your criminal defense attorney can assist you in seeking an agreement with the prosecution and the court for you to be admitted into an Oklahoma Diversion Programs in your county.

Although failure in any Diversion Program described above may result in being incarcerated, the majority of participants in these programs would be facing jury trial or prison if they did not agree to participate in these programs. Successful completion in almost any diversion program results in the case being dismissed.

Please see a detailed explanation of the most common diversion programs in Oklahoma below:

Veterans' Diversion Program

Veteran Diversion Programs are only available to service members who currently or previously served in the United States Military. These programs are intended to prevent Veterans from serving jail or prison time, while receiving treatment and the regiment they lived while in the service. Veteran diversion programs are one of the few programs that accept violent offenders.

The service record of every potential participant must be collected and reviewed prior to admission into any veteran diversion programs. This is usually accomplished by the program submitting a DD-214 request to the Department of Veterans Affairs. Upon service verification, the participant will attend formation for the veteran program; participate in treatment; and participate in job counseling.

Veterans Court

Some counties that do not offer Veteran Diversion Programs, where the case is dismissed upon admittance to the program, offer Veterans Court. Veterans Courts follow the Drug Court model, in which you enter a plea to your charges and accept a specific outcome in your case, if you are not successful in the program. However, if you successfully complete Veterans Court, according to the program staff, then your case will be dismissed at the end of the program. This is an intensive program and should only be entered into after careful consideration.

As a combat veteran, I am a Fierce Advocate® for veteran diversion programs. We owe it to those that have offered their lives to give them every opportunity to be successful. All veteran diversion programs aim to reestablish order, mental health, address substance abuse issues, and assist veterans' return to productive lives. You should discuss this diversion option with your criminal defense attorney, if you have served in the United States Military, including the National Guard, and you are facing criminal charges in Oklahoma.

DUI Court & Drug Court

Drug Court and DUI Court are the most prevalent Diversion Programs in Oklahoma. Drug Court is specifically authorized by statute at Oklahoma Statutes Title 22, beginning at Section 471. These programs are intensive outpatient treatment courts that have the primary purpose of diverting defendants that would otherwise be sentenced to prison. Additionally, these treatment programs are focused on alcohol and drug treatment to address the specific needs of each defendant.

Participation in Drug Court and DUI Court are options; however, in some instances the last chance to avoid prison on a case is to participate in one of these treatment courts. All participants in Drug Court and DUI Court are required to submit to drug and alcohol testing, appear at treatment court, participate in treatment and counseling, and maintain employment. As a participant progresses through the treatment court, their liberties will increase and responsibilities to the program decrease.

At least 73 of the 77 counties in Oklahoma offer drug court diversion programs. The benefits of participating in diversion is obvious, eventual dismissal of your case; however, the consequences are equally apparent. Failure of DUI Court or Drug Court can result in being sent to prison. It is important to work with your criminal defense attorney to ensure you understand the terms of your treatment court contract, as it will explain the consequences of a violation or termination from the program.

DUI Court and Drug Court are not one strike programs. There is some grace for falling off the wagon; however, mistakes have consequences. Although the goal of these diversion programs is complete abstinence, in most cases you will receive a sanction, including jail time, for violating program rules before being sentenced to prison. You should discuss this diversion option and all other options with your criminal defense attorney, prior to entering into any contract.

Mental Health Court

Most families have been touched by some form of mental health issues, and many times offenders suffer from mental health problems. Mental Health Courts were established to provide diagnosis and experienced treatment for offenders that suffer from mental health issues, short of those offenders being sentenced to prison.

It is estimated that fifty-five percent (55%) of all Oklahoma offenders have a history of or are currently suffering symptoms of poor mental health, which does not include the thousands of offenders without documented mental health issues. Some Oklahoma criminal courts have begun to respond to prevalence of mental health issues in the criminal justice system by establishing these treatment courts, which are similar to Drug Court.

Treatment for mental health works in most cases and can greatly reduce the likelihood of re-offending. At least 14 counties out of the 77 counties in Oklahoma operate Mental Health Courts. Mental Health Courts provide the following to participants: mental health evaluations, treatment, counseling, employment opportunities, and assistance in seeking disability resources.

Successful completion of Mental Health Court results in your case being dismissed; however, like Drug Court, if you fail the program you will likely be sentenced to prison. If you or your loved one is facing our justice system and have a history of mental health, you should explore the option of applying to Mental Health Court. Your criminal defense attorney can advise you if such a program is available in the county where your case is pending and whether or not it is a good option or possible resolution for your case.

Re-Merge Program

Re-Merge is another comprehensive treatment program. It is for female offenders only and is designed to assist mothers and pregnant offenders in transforming from being on the verge of prison to being productive and employed citizens in the community. The mission statement of Re-Merge says it best:

> ReMerge is a female diversion program for mothers and pregnant women facing prison in Oklahoma. This diversion program works with the Department of Corrections & Department of Mental Health and Substance Abuse Services to find treatment and diversion options for women facing prison. ReMerge, similar to Drug Court, uses treatment to address mental health, behavior health, substance abuse, trauma, and poverty.

Upon successful completion of ReMerge, the participant's felony is dismissed, they will have a job, they will be in stable housing, and will be participating in an ongoing treatment plan. ReMerge's comprehensive plan boasts a five percent (5%) recidivism rate, which means only five-percent of graduates re-offend! You should discuss this diversion option with your criminal defense attorney, if you or your loved one qualify for ReMerge. We have many clients that have successfully turned their life around with the assistance of this program.

Delayed Sentencing for Young Adults

Research shows young offenders have a substantially higher chance of turning their life around and not re-offending. Therefore, the Delayed Sentencing Program for Young Adults was created for young offenders. Delayed Sentencing, or Regimented Inmate Discipline Program (RID), is a boot camp program for criminal defendants between the age of eighteen (18) and twenty-five (25), which is a serious Diversion Program giving participants a roughly year-long taste of prison, for the opportunity to avoid a straight prison sentence.

Individuals must enter a plea before their twenty-sixth (26th) birthday to participate in the program, and cannot be charged with any of the violent felonies listed in Oklahoma Statutes Title 22

Section 996.1. This Diversion Program is not for the faint at heart and typically should not be explored for non-serious felonies. However, it is a great program between simple probation and a prison sentence.

RID has an in-custody option and an out-of-custody option (far fewer participants). After a criminal defendant enters a plea; they will participate in the regimented program for a period between six months to eighteen months. Upon completion of the program or termination from the program, a report is generated that details how the defendant performed. Poor performance or failure of RID can result in a felony conviction and prison. Alternatively, successful completion can result in dismissal of charges or probation, including deferred sentence (not a conviction).

You should discuss this diversion option with your criminal defense attorney if you or your loved one are facing criminal charges and you are under the age of twenty-six.

Community Sentencing

Community Sentencing is an intensive supervised probation program that is more intensive than any other probation program. However, it is not a diversion court, i.e. you will not have additional court appearances after entering Community Sentencing. Rather, if you are admitted into the program, you will be required to meet with your probation officer on a regular basis and complete a number of probation requirements for the first six to eighteen months of probation.

Community sentencing is a very good option for offenders with criminal history that do not qualify for one of the above referenced treatment courts or programs. Successful completion of Community Sentencing takes dedication and commitment to stay the course. However, most offenders that successfully complete the program have a lower likelihood to re-offend (get in trouble again) and are in a better place than where their case began. Again, the alternative to this program for many defendants is prison; therefore, if a client can be successful in the program it may be the last option to avoid prison time.

Community Sentencing Act, Oklahoma Statutes Title 22, beginning at Section 988.1 provides the following mission statement:

Community Sentencing is an alternative to prison for criminal defendants with a prior felony conviction or multiple felony convictions, even some violent crime convictions.

In order to participate in Community Sentencing, you must be eligible for the program. The first step in determining program eligibility is an assessment: either an "Offender Screening" or a "Level of Services Inventory" (LSI), which gives the parties insight or a forecast of the likelihood of success for the individual. The LSI results in an eligibility score that is similar to "Goldilocks"; you must need more services than probation; however, you cannot need so many services that it is likely you will fail the program. Either way, your criminal defense attorney can advocate for you to be admitted into the program. However, the parties must all agree, or you will not be admitted.

Although successful completion of Community Sentencing will not result in dismissal of charges; it will result in not going to prison. You should discuss this prison diversion option with your criminal defense attorney, if you or your loved one has one or more felony convictions and is facing new felony charges in Oklahoma.

Alternative Programs for Youth

The juvenile justice system is primarily focused on treatment for minors and getting them in a place that reduces the likelihood that they will re-offend. Research indicates that youth have a very high chance of not getting in trouble again, if they receive treatment and guidance to address their needs. The juvenile system provides minors facing criminal trouble an opportunity to avoid the common consequences: criminal charges, conviction, and incarceration.

The First-Time Offender Program helps youth avoid criminal charges. This program, like most, is run by individual counties. The Skills Education Program (SEP) exists in Oklahoma County. The SEP is a sixteen-hour course, in which an individual youth and his or her parent work to develop proper responses to anger and conflict. Eligibility for this program requires one of the following: 1) behavior exhibited at school or home that concerns parents or teachers; or 2) a youth that is arrested for a first-time criminal offense.

After a criminal allegation is made against a juvenile, but before charges are filed, a youth may enter into other Diversion Programs by agreement with the District Attorney's Office through coordinating with the juvenile intake officer in Diversion Services Unit or the Community Intervention Center CIC.

All three of these options connect youths and their family with services to find better responses to controversy. You should discuss these youth diversion options with your criminal defense attorney, if you have a loved one that is facing juvenile justice.

Although Oklahoma still incarcerates more men and women than nearly any place on earth per capita, when you work with an experienced criminal defense attorney you greatly increase the chance of minimizing your exposure to the worst outcomes in our system, being sent to prison. Your attorney's experience and knowledge surrounding these issues and identifying your treatment needs is very important to the outcome of your case. Do not give up hope or accept prison as an outcome of any case, until you and your criminal defense attorney have explored all available options.

COMMON CRIMES CHARGED IN OKLAHOMA

"Cannon & Associates represented me for a situation that could have easily sent me to prison, I am currently on probation and the associates at Cannon & Associates worked together as a team, working hard and diligent on my case. Today was my sentencing date and Tom Stone and his team were able to get the case thrown out with me only having to pay court fees, God is good All the time! I will refer this team to anyone needing an attorney, and this will definitely be my family attorney from here on out. Thank you to my amazing Team of experts at Cannon & Associates."

Joshua

The purpose of this section is to give you a general sense of the criminal justice systems in Oklahoma. In order for you and your family to be better prepared to face our criminal justice system, it is relevant to discuss some of the most common criminal offenses in Oklahoma and general guidance for each. The most prevalent criminal offenses in Oklahoma are detailed in the following section of this chapter, along with specific guidance.

The final caveat to this section is that nothing can match specific legal advice to your situation from an experienced criminal defense attorney, and you should obtain it as soon as possible from the best criminal defense attorney possible.

However, until you meet with an attorney at Cannon & Associates, the following guidance to the five most common types of criminal charges in Oklahoma will hopefully be helpful to you:

- Drug Crimes
- Driving under the Influence of Alcohol (DUI)
- Assault & Battery Crimes
- Property Crimes
- White Collar Crimes

DRUG CRIMES IN OKLAHOMA

"I highly recommend Cannon & Associates to anyone in need of an attorney for any reason. If they are unable to take your case they assist you in finding someone who can. I want to personally thank Kelly Byrd for her quick response in helping me and my family get the attorney we needed and the continued contact to make sure we were doing well. That true care for people is hard to find in attorney's and this law firm absolutely cares ☐ ☐THANK YOU SO VERY MUCH!!"

Sara

Those facing criminal charges related to drugs in Oklahoma have a broad spectrum of backgrounds and circumstances that resulted in them facing drug charges. Defendants facing drug charges range from first time drug users and passengers in a vehicle that contained drugs to habitual users and those accused of trafficking drugs.

The variety of drug offenses someone can face in the criminal justice system, are as broad as the circumstances that result in someone being charged in the first place. Most drug offenses fall under one of the following categories:

- Possession of Drug Paraphernalia
- Possession of Drugs
- Possession of Drugs with the Intent to Distribute
- Possession of Drug Proceeds
- Drug Trafficking
- Conspiracy to Commit one of these offenses

Drug crimes are taken seriously by prosecutors, from simple possession to complex drug trafficking and racketeering schemes. Unfortunately, a large percentage of state prisoners are incarcerated based on drug crimes.

Facing drug charges can impact your freedom, your finances, and your future. Drug charges carry more than a potential prison sentence; they potentially carry substantial fines, difficult probation, and complex counseling or treatment programs. Unfortunately, the harshest punishment in drug cases is often the lasting effect on your record and career. A conviction may appear on background checks and make it difficult to obtain employment, loans, and professional licenses. It is essential to obtain quality legal representation from an Oklahoma drug crime defense attorney that has experience both fighting / identifying issues in the government's case, as well as obtaining the best possible outcome for each client's circumstance.

You need an experienced criminal defense attorney who will fight for you, if you have been arrested, charged, or you are being investigated for any drug offense. As will be discussed in more detail below, drug charges come in many forms, and each type of case requires a different approach in order to obtain the best possible outcome.

Possession of Drug Paraphernalia

Possession of drug paraphernalia is an allegation that you possessed an instrument used to carry, weigh, or consume an illegal drug. Possession of drug paraphernalia is often charged in addition to the underlying drug offense, without affording you the defense of double punishment for one event.

Another often overlooked and widely contested area of drug defense is possession of drug proceeds. Anything law enforcement believes is purchased from the sale of drugs can be categorized as drug proceeds, including but not limited to the following: homes, cars, motorcycles, televisions, electronics, drug paraphernalia, items used in the creation or storage of drugs, equipment used in the cultivation, production, or transportation of drugs, as well as your money, whether cash or in a bank account.

Fortunately, this crime is a misdemeanor. However, it can result in jail time or a substantial fine. An experienced defense attorney may be able to show that insufficient evidence exists to support you possessed the alleged paraphernalia or that it was not in fact used for an illicit purpose.

Possession of Drug Proceeds

This "drug" offense alleges possession of funds or property that was obtained in connection with illegal drug transactions. In order to be charged and convicted of possession of drug proceeds, the prosecution must prove a connection between the item of value and drugs. Specifically, knowingly acquiring, receiving goods, or derived from a violation of the Dangerous Substance Act.

These charges are subject to overreach and often used to support asset forfeiture actions, in which the government moves to take your property based on its connection to illegal actions. An experienced defense attorney can hold the government to its burden and help you.

Misdemeanor Possession of Drugs

Prior to July of 2017, being charged with possession of even a very small amount of a controlled substance would result in a felony case. This was true even with no prior criminal record. Fortunately, drug laws changed in Oklahoma making simple possession of drugs no longer a felony offense. This is now true, even if you have prior felony charges or convictions for possession of drugs. Possession of drugs carries up to one year in jail and up to a $1,000 fine for first time offenders, which is a serious potential consequence; however, it is far less than five years in prison.

Possession with Intent to Distribute

Possession with Intent to Distribute drugs is a felony and carries prison time. Whenever an individual is arrested with drugs that the prosecutor believes is more than personal use or the person has drug paraphernalia, such as multiple baggies, a scale, or other items that indicate dividing or selling drugs; that person will likely be arrested and charged with felony possession with intent to distribute.

The accusation of distributing drugs to others is taken very seriously by prosecutors, as it goes beyond addiction / personal consumption to an enterprise related to drugs. In addition to carrying large fines and collateral consequences, a defendant may be faced with the potential of life in prison even on a first offense.

No minimum or maximum amount of a specific drug are set forth in Oklahoma statutes to quantify distribution of drugs. Rather, it is primarily a totality of the circumstances analysis, meaning if a prosecutor believes you may be sharing drugs or selling drugs then you will be charged with distribution.

An experienced criminal defense attorney can fight to suppress evidence in your case, if law enforcement violated your rights in accessing the drugs, i.e., officers did not have a basis to conduct a traffic stop or search that resulted in discovery drugs. Additionally, an experience drug defense attorney may be able to build a narrative to support the argument that you were not distributing drugs, but simply in possession of drugs or using them.

Drug Trafficking

Due to the popularity of television shows on the cartel and drug trafficking, most people understand the term drug trafficking and that it is taken very seriously by law enforcement and prosecutors. However, what many people do not know is that you can be charged with drug trafficking for being in possession of far less than a truckload of drugs.

Many of our clients and their families have a difficult time distinguishing possession with intent to distribute and drug trafficking. However, the distinction is very simple. Drug Trafficking is based on the weight of drugs, and the distribution is implied or understood, simply based on the amount of the drugs. Alternatively, possession with intent to distribute requires proof or evidence of an intent to distribute the drugs. The volume of drugs necessary to constitute trafficking is based upon the specific drug in question.

Drug trafficking in Oklahoma, as is the case in most states, is dependent upon a threshold or minimum amount or weight of drugs that law enforcement believes can be tied directly to a single defendant. The volume amounting to Trafficking for some of the most common drugs is as follows:

- Marijuana: 25 pounds
- Methamphetamine: 20 ounces
- Cocaine: 28 grams
- Heroin: 10 grams
- Ecstasy or MDMA: 10 grams or 30 pills
- Hydrocodone: 3,750 grams
- Oxycodone: 400 grams
- Morphine: 1,000 grams
- LSD or Acid: 1 gram
- Benzodiazepine: 500 grams

Aggravated Drug Trafficking

Aggravated drug trafficking is the most serious drug offense in Oklahoma and carries up to life in prison. The offense, as is the case in simple trafficking, is based solely on the amount of the drugs found. Aggravated trafficking requires a testable amount of drugs that is far greater than the amounts described above for trafficking drugs.

Aggravated drug trafficking is an 85% crime in Oklahoma, meaning if you are sentenced to prison, you will be required to serve 85% of your sentence prior to release. The exact penalty for drug trafficking and distribution depends on the specific type of drug and amount or volume of drugs involved. The penalty can include up to life in prison for these offenses, and up to half-a-million dollar fine.

Drug Schedules in America: Defining Drugs

All drugs, whether inherently legal or illegal, fall under one of five Drug Schedules determined by the Drug Enforcement Agency of the United States, the DEA. This list includes the most dangerous illegal drugs all the way down to common prescription medicine.

Schedule I: this category of drugs has no federally accepted medicinal purpose and has the highest potential for drug abuse, ie no doctor can lawfully prescribe these drugs. Schedule I includes drugs such as: marijuana, heroin, LSD (acid), MDMA (ecstasy), mushrooms, and many more.

Schedule II: this category of drugs has minimal accepted medical purposes and those that are accepted are highly regulated due to the high likelihood for abuse and addiction for these drugs, including: cocaine, morphine, codeine, other opioids, other painkillers, and opium.

Schedule III: the drugs in this category have a lower risk of being abused and the threat of illicit use are moderate. There are many acceptable medicinal uses for these drugs. Some of the drugs falling under Schedule III are hormones, narcotic compounds, anabolic steroids, and barbiturates.

Schedule IV: this category includes drugs with very common medical purposes and a lower risk for abuse than the preceding three schedules, such as Ambien, Ephedrine, Klonopin, Valium, and Xanax.

Schedule V: this category is reserved for drugs which the DEA believes have the lowest likelihood of abuse, i.e. these drugs are not stimulants or depressants and contain a low number of narcotics.

Defense in Drug Cases

As discussed in previous chapters, the prospect of obtaining a positive result in criminal cases involving drug charges is greatly increased with hiring criminal defense counsel with experience defending drug cases. There are two avenues of defense in every drug case to explore: mitigating/extenuating circumstances that led to your getting in trouble, and legal defenses including, lack of evidence to support the case against you/evaluating whether any of your rights were violated. Working with an experienced criminal defense team will assist you in identifying the best courses of action to pursue in your defense.

An important step in any drug defense, unless you are set on fighting your case, is to identify the most appropriate treatment or rehabilitation program, while your case is pending. By identifying and participating in a treatment option that is appropriate for your circumstance, you increase the likelihood of obtaining a positive outcome in your case.

Additionally, many drug defense cases involve search and seizure issues that allow an experienced defense attorney to seek to exclude evidence from your case based on law enforcement violating your rights. This process is called suppression of evidence, and (is) a complex process, including review of all evidence, legal research, and fighting in court for suppression of evidence. You should only work with a defense attorney with experience in suppression hearings if you are fighting a legal issue in your drug case.

In many cases, if you have been proactive in working with your defense attorney, you may be able to resolve your case for less serious charges than the originally filed charges. Anytime you can resolve your case under less serious charges you increase the likelihood of less punishment, and getting the experience behind you sooner.

DRIVING UNDER THE INFLUENCE

"Counsel John Cannon was flawless in every way in my case. Defendant & family had so much first-time fears about the court process, etc. due to this client's first time ever DUI crime, at the age of 60 years old. Thankfully attorney John Cannon could not have more perfectly represented this client. 100% referral suggested!! Highly so."

Hubert

Criminal allegations related to a motor vehicle and consuming alcohol are some of the most common offenses in state court. These offenses include a wide variety of circumstances that are covered by the following offenses: Driving under the Influence of Alcohol (DUI); Driving While Impaired (DWI); or Being in Actual Physical Control while under the Influence (APC).

When charged with a DUI or related offense you are facing the potential of jail time, lost employment opportunities, substantial probation, court costs, as well as the potential loss of your driving privilege.

DUI: the evidence necessary to support a DUI prosecution is in the title of the offense, the prosecutor must prove that you were driving and that you were intoxicated, while driving. As simple as that sounds, the science and defenses that exist in DUI cases are highly complex. The evidence sufficient to support a DUI conviction is complex and you increase your chances of a positive outcome by working with an experienced DUI defense attorney.

APC: the prosecution must show that you had the immediate ability to control/drive a motor vehicle, that you were intoxicated, and that you were on or adjacent to a public road, in order to support a conviction for Actual Physical Control of a Motor Vehicle.

These cases often involve complex search and seizure issues, as law enforcement must have a valid basis for coming in contact with someone in a motor vehicle, which allows experienced criminal defense attorneys an avenue to seek suppression of evidence in many APC cases.

Defending DUI and APC cases

As discussed in previous chapters, your chances for obtaining the best possible outcome in your criminal case or, specifically, your DUI case is greatly impact by the caliber of the attorney that defends your case. Your chances of forming the best strategy in your DUI case increase greatly when you work with a DUI defense attorney with substantial experience identifying and addressing the issues common to these cases.

Working with an experienced criminal defense team will assist you in identifying the best courses of action to pursue in your DUI or APC defense. An important step in any DUI defense, unless you are set on fighting your case, is to work with your defense team to identify the probation and treatment requirements and be proactive in completing those steps. When you complete the work ahead of time, it will assist your defense counsel in obtaining the best possible outcome for you.

Alternatively, you need to work with a defense attorney that knows how to fight DUI cases if you were wrongly stopped by law enforcement and/or you are not guilty of DUI. Therefore, you want to collect all the evidence available, including dash camera and body camera footage by law enforcement, all incident reports, police call logs, witness statements, tests conducted, and any other available information.

Knowledge is power in evaluating the strength of your suppression issue or defense. When you work with an experienced DUI defense attorney, you will have a better opportunity to evaluate your defense and plan how to attack your case.

This area of criminal defense is one of the most complicated in any jurisdiction. DUI and similar charges, the underlying legal principals, and the administrative action related to your driver's license make DUI defense highly complex. Please see the separate chapters on DUI and IDAP for more detailed information about important considerations in the area of DUI defense.

DUI and Your Driver's License

The complex issues related to driver's license privileges and DUI will be discussed in great detail in a later chapter; however, for now, it is important to note that you will have a separate issue related to retaining your driver's license following a DUI, which must be handled at the same time as your criminal case.

Your driver's license is governed by the Department of Public Safety (DPS) and you must either initiate a district court appeal to fight your driver's license revocation or apply to a diversion program immediately. These issues will be addressed in detail in the following chapters on Driver's License and DPS & IDAP.

ASSAULT & BATTERY CRIMES IN OKLAHOMA

"Very professional and detailed. They responded promptly and gave me all the information I needed to make my decisions."
Sharena

Another very common area of criminal charges are offenses that fall under assault and battery crimes. In Oklahoma, there are a wide variety of assault and battery crimes, each with its own legal elements, facts to constitute the crime, and potential punishment. From bar fights to domestic violence, to homicides, assault and battery crimes cover a wide variety of conflicts; however, their defenses and overall framework have substantial overlap.

This section is intended to give you a framework for this category of crimes and how to prepare to defend yourself if you are facing a criminal charge for assault and battery. Prior to addressing specific assault and battery crimes, it is important to have a working understanding of what each of these terms means in the legal context:

Assault: the threat to induce physical harm on another person – which must include a physical action, including but not limited to moving aggressively towards a person. Assault does not include physical contact with another person.

Battery: the intentional use of force against another person that causes an amount of harm. The amount and source of the force separates many of the different battery crimes. In order to constitute a battery, physical contact must be made between the victim and defendant.

Stated another way, assault is the act of threatening force and battery is the completion of the threat or the actual use of force. The relationship between the parties and the amount/type of forced used is the primary indicator of what assault and battery crime has occurred. With this information, you can safely speculate as to your charges, if you know what the allegations are against you.

Types of Assault and Battery Crimes

There are more categories of assault and battery crimes than any other area of offenses in our justice system. This section will not cover every assault and battery offense; however, it is illustrative of the range of offenses, what the prosecutor must prove for each offense, and the potential consequences of the most common offenses:

Simple Assault is a misdemeanor, which requires the prosecution prove a threat of physical force, and carries minimal jail-time. Assault charges are rarely filed on their own as it is difficult to prove to a jury that one person's fear of a battery was justified.

Simple Assault & Battery is a misdemeanor, which requires the prosecutor to prove the defendant struck another individual in a harmful manner. It does not require an injury to the victim, only use of force resulting in contact. Assault and battery charges are filed regularly and typically are the result of a fight between two unrelated individuals. We defend simple assault and battery cases by contacting the alleged victim and determining whether or not the government can make their case.

Domestic Assault & Battery is a misdemeanor offense, which requires the prosecutor show a party battered another person, with whom they share a qualifying domestic relationship. Due to the prevalence of a gradual escalation of violence in domestic relationships, substantial consequences and terms of probation can follow these types of cases.

We defend domestic violence cases by identifying the involved parties, determining what the parties want to see as an outcome in the case, and either working towards that goal or potentially fighting the case by requiring the government to prove domestic violence occurred. Domestic violence cases are as complex as DUI defense and require working with a very experienced defense attorney in order to balance all the interests at issue and obtain the best outcome, whether it is dismissal of charges, fighting the case, or reaching an agreed resolution.

Strangulation is a felony offense that is taken very seriously by prosecutors, based on the escalation of violence and potential death that may come as the result of strangulation. However, this offense is charged against many defendants when a lesser offense is more appropriate. In strangulation cases, our clients are facing serious risk of prison time, therefore, it is very important to identify an early plan of attack to defend these cases.

Assault & Battery Great Bodily Injury is a felony offense that implies long lasting injury or protracted / permanent disfigurement. The injuries in these cases are very serious and the punishment sought by prosecutors is equally harsh. In defending these cases, we strive to identify our client's narrative and develop a treatment plan to show a similar event will not reoccur, while we fight for the best outcome possible.

Assault & Battery with a Dangerous Weapon is a felony, which involves someone being battered by an object controlled by the defendant, rather than a punch or a kick. Some of the most common events that give rise to this charge include stabbings with any object, and a person being struck by a hard object, such as a bat.

Objects may be dangerous by the manner in which they are used, ie a "weapon" in the traditional sense is not required. Prosecutors typically see defendants with this charge as a substantial threat and often seek substantial punishment. In defense of these cases, we try to build our client's narrative that explains or mitigates the circumstances that led to the offense, as well as fighting for clients.

Assault & Battery with a Deadly Weapon is a felony, which is largely indistinguishable from assault and battery with a dangerous weapon, except this offense requires a "deadly weapon" as defined by statute. A deadly weapon is an object meant to inflict harsh bodily injury, such as a gun or a sharp object. However, other objects can be charged as deadly weapons based on the manner they are allegedly used. Any object that can disfigure, break bones, or kill qualifies as a deadly weapon. This is one of the most serious assault and battery crimes and prosecutors almost always seek lengthy prison sentences for these offenses.

Sexual Assault and Battery Offenses are felony offenses, which allege a person engaged in a sexual act or sexual proposition without the consent of another party, or that party lacked the ability to form consent. Other than homicides, no assault and battery offenses are treated more harshly than sexual assault cases. It is vital to retain an experienced sexual assault defense attorney immediately. Your defense counsel can work with investigators, a polygrapher, and counselors to help build the narrative of your defense and seek the best outcome for you. Your future depends on the caliber defense attorney you hire in the most serious of cases.

Homicide, Manslaughter, and Murder these offenses all have the underlying element of loss of life and are all felonies, except negligent homicide. Prosecutors look harshly on these offenses and seek lengthy prison sentences, including life in prison, if they believe a defendant willfully took the life of another person. It is crucial to have experienced criminal defense counsel that has handled multiple homicide, manslaughter, and murder cases to ensure your rights are protected and you receive the best defense possible.

Your counsel must begin building your defense immediately by obtaining all evidence and working with an investigator to build your defense. Being charged with any assault and battery crime, especially a felony, will expose you or your loved one to a real risk of going to prison. Many other potential consequences coincide with the risk of prison in serious assault and battery crimes, including difficult probation, restitution, and employment consequences.

It is important to know your rights, the potential consequences you face on your specific assault and battery charges, and to retain an experienced criminal defense attorney that has successfully defended your specific type of offense in the past. Your life and freedom are on the line, you must invest in the best defense.

PROPERTY CRIMES IN OKLAHOMA

"John Cannon did an awesome job in my friend's DUI defense. He addressed all of her fears and explained everything! John truly cares and saved her driver's license. I can't give him a higher recommendation."

Marshall

Property crimes are another very common type of criminal offense charged in state court. Property crimes cover a wide range of offenses that focus on someone taking or damaging something that does not belong to them. Property crimes involve theft or damage to the belongings of someone else and come with a wide variety of serious consequences.

The seriousness of the potential punishment for a specific property crime comes from the value of the property and also the manner in which it was taken or destroyed, i.e. stealing property that is left out has far less serious consequences than property taken by force or fear. The most common property crimes are listed below:

Burglary: entering a building, structure, or vehicle for the purpose of committing a crime, including theft. Burglary is characterized as a property crime based on the breaking and entering of the property without permission, not the subsequent crime or attempted crime. Breaking and entering the location is a necessary element of burglary, otherwise the offense is a trespass.

Robbery: taking property from another person by force or fear constitutes robbery and is a violent crime. Intimidation, fear, or actual force are necessary elements of robbery; otherwise, the offense is simply theft, which is far less serous. Prosecutors treat robbery offenses very seriously and the punishments can be upwards of twenty years. Therefore, it is vital that you obtain the best defense attorney possible to fight for your freedom and future.

Larceny: taking or moving property without authority is larceny. Surprisingly, a much larger range than the common understanding of larceny is sufficient for a conviction. It is important you understand the evidence necessary for a prosecutor to prove larceny prior to accepting an offer. Additionally, larceny offenses may be a misdemeanor or felony. The punishment range is typically based on the value of the property taken. Therefore, do not accept the property taken is sufficient for felony larceny, unless you know the prosecution can make its case for felony larceny.

Unauthorized Use of a Motor Vehicle: the title of this offense is a simple explanation for this common felony related to automobiles. When a person uses, takes, or moves a vehicle without proper authority, it may constitute felony Unauthorized Use of a Motor Vehicle (UUMV). This category of offenses includes grand theft auto, as well as joyriding, which is a misdemeanor offense. It is important to understand the specific requirements for the prosecutor to make a case of UUMV against you versus joyriding, prior to resolving your case as a felony.

Arson: an uncommon but well-known property crime is arson. It is the act of causing damage to property by fire or some other incendiary. The facts surrounding an arson offense, specifically what led to the fire starting, plays a major role in how serious the offense will be seen by the prosecutor.

Some of the most important questions relate to the categories expressed above, how much property damage was done, and whether any people were harmed or placed in harm's way. Allegedly burning down an apartment complex is handled far more seriously than burning the old shed in a neighbor's yard. Trust me, I've represented people facing both allegations.

Vandalism: a common offense that captures the same conduct as arson; however, no fire or incendiary is involved. Vandalism can be filed as a misdemeanor or a felony. The value and extent of the damage plays a major role in how serious the charges.

Property crimes can span from near accident with little punishment to very serious offenses with potentially life changing consequences. How severely a property crime is prosecuted dependent upon the value of the property in question and the amount of force, coercion, fraud, or fear allegedly used in the act.

It is important to know your rights and retain an Oklahoma criminal defense attorney with experience defending property crimes as soon as possible. In addition to your freedom and reputation being on the line, a felony property crime may deprive you of civil rights: owning or being in the presence of a firearm, voting, holding office, employment/housing, and cause difficulty in obtaining a loan or mortgage, and other penalties.

We have successfully represented clients facing every type of property crime and can help you find your way through the process ahead. Whatever counsel you choose, be sure to get a clear understanding of what the prosecution is required to prove in your case, the consequences you face, as well as a strategy to defend your property crime case.

In the end, there are two main approaches to defending a property crime in Oklahoma: an innocence defense or, admission of the act, but defense of the reason or mitigation of the offense. An innocence defense consists of developing your story, identifying witnesses and evidence to support your defense, and attacking the credibility of all eyewitness identification and law enforcement investigation.

In a case where you cannot contest you committed the act, there are several legal and factual defenses available to you: protecting yourself by self-defense, defense of another, which removes your culpability; accident, or mistake of fact i.e., accidental entry to the wrong property, inability to form the requisite intent due to intoxication; and a number of other mitigating and extenuating circumstances. It is important to hire an experienced criminal defense attorney for your property crime defense that has knowledge of property law and defenses available in your case.

WHITE COLLAR CRIME

"My attorney at Cannon & Associates has went above and beyond to make sure all matters were taken care of. I stay about 5 hours away and he made sure to keep me updated through calls and other communications. His paralegal Ms. Brittany done an excellent job answering questions and making sure I could speak with Mr. Stone as needed. The whole team is very helpful and they even have accommodating payment options. I give Cannon & Associates two thumbs up."

Henry

White collar crime is the final common type of criminal offense charged in state court that this section will cover. White collar crimes are similar to property crimes; however, they do not involve force, threat, or violence. White collar crimes are primarily acts of acquiring property or assets through fraud, deceit, or abuse of authority.

The seriousness and resulting potential punishment of white-collar crime is based on the value of the property and the number of victims impacted. Some white-collar offenses include acts against the government resulting in millions of dollars of loss. These offenses are handled at the federal level in most cases. Alternatively, the majority of white-collar crime is at the local level, involving allegations of employees and managers wrongfully taking from a business.

Most white-collar offenses fall under fraud or theft. Fraud is an act or scheme of deceit with the intent to deprive or receive an unjustified gain or monetary compensation, ie lying to obtain something. Theft is simply the taking of something the person is not entitled to by a variety of actions. However, in order to remain characterized as white-collar crime, no force or violence can be used. The majority of white-collar offenses are felonies and carry potential prison time.

The effects of being charged or convicted of a white-collar crime can have lifelong consequences. Restitution (money to compensate a victim for their loss) is a substantial factor in white collar crime, as the amounts can be tens or hundreds of thousands of dollars. In some cases, a defendant's ability to pay restitution can result in avoiding prison or even a felony conviction.

An additional concern with restitution in white collar offenses is the authority for the court to order treble damages (three times the victim's loss) as restitution. In contested restitution hearings, courts often enter orders far above the loss alleged by the victim. Therefore, you want to ensure you have a solid argument to contest the alleged restitution and a Fierce Advocate® on your side, if you are contesting restitution in your case.

An experienced white-collar defense attorney can potentially greatly reduce the amount of restitution you will be obligated to pay through accounting and detailed review of the alleged loss. Forensic accounting and/or experienced review of the financials of your case by your defense team may even be able to have your case reduced from a felony to a misdemeanor if the actual loss falls below the threshold for a felony. The following are the most common white-collar offenses:

White Collar Crimes of Fraud

Forgery: the process of fraudulently signing the signature or authorization of another for financial gain. The most common forms of forgery involve signing the signature of another person to slips, contracts, checks, and authorizations that were not and would not be authorized by the responsible party, which is done for any unauthorized purpose.

Tax Fraud: the title of this offense says it all, tax fraud is the act of misrepresenting your income or tax liability by deceit. Criminal charges for tax fraud typically requires more than mistakes on your tax return. The elements of this offense require an intent to commit the wrong. Therefore, one of the most powerful defenses in tax fraud cases is to build a clear explanation of how the mistakes in taxes took place. However, if criminal intent is obvious, mitigating the circumstance and seeking resolution is the best course of action.

Computer Fraud/Scam: computers are linked to the internet and the majority of these offenses are prosecuted in federal court, under the interstate commerce clause. When someone uses a computer network, such as a social media network to obtain someone's property by deceit, this offense is frequently charged.

Mail Fraud: everyone has received unsolicited mail; however, those mailers can become a crime, if they seek property or money from the recipient by misleading or lying to the recipient of the mail. These offenses are typically prosecuted in federal court and reserved for offenses involving multiple victims or hundreds of thousands of dollars in damages.

Credit Card/Securities Fraud Bank Fraud: similar to tax fraud, this offense occurs when a defendant misrepresents something to a credit card company or bank, ie claiming fraudulent charges, which were knowingly expended by the customer. The majority of these events are handled internally through collections. However, when these charges are filed, it typically relates to a substantial sum of alleged damages.

White Collar Crimes of Theft

Embezzlement: an act of taking property or funds that belong to someone else or an entity without authority. Embezzlement is one of the most common forms of "white-collar crime", which is a category of taking funds or property from a business or business client without authority, i.e. an act of larceny by trick or abuse of authority.

Extortion: commonly referred to as blackmail, extortion is the act of threatening, but not performing, an act of violence or the release of damaging information, in exchange for funds or services. Business owners and executives are often the victim of alleged extortion. These offenses are typically prosecuted in federal court and can result in substantial prison sentences, if convicted.

Counterfeiting: the act of making bills or other currency without authorization and holding those bills out as real currency. The technology to print tender that looks like real bills has increased dramatically, and these offenses are taken very seriously and prosecuted in federal court. You need an experienced federal criminal defense attorney, if you are facing allegations of counterfeiting.

Identify Theft: the act of using the identity of another actual person to obtain property, credit, or something else of value can constitute identity theft. When someone is charged with this offense they have usually been caught in the act and must seek to mitigate the circumstance to avoid jail or a conviction. However, cases of innocence do exist, in which a skilled criminal defense attorney must build a defense to explain the false accusation.

Tax evasion: the allegation of intentionally avoiding paying taxes by outright failing to pay taxes. The penalties for this offense vary dependent upon the duration and amount of tax evasion.

Money Laundering: the act of "washing" funds, or taking illegally obtained funds and running them through a legitimate business in order to enter the funds into the market through a lawful channel. These offenses almost always coincide with prosecution for an underlying criminal act or enterprise. Either way, if you are facing money laundering charges, it is vital that you obtain a Fierce Advocate® to fight for your future and freedom.

You or your loved one need an experienced criminal defense team if accused or charged with a white-collar crime. Cannon & Associates may be Your Fierce Advocate® and will help you in evaluating the evidence and finances involved in your case to determine your best course of action in defending your white-collar case.

DUI: KNOW YOUR OPTIONS

"I had Dalton as a lawyer and Brittany as the paralegal that was helping me with my case and they both did a great job. Very friendly, nice guy. Really pleased with the outcome Dalton was able to get me in court. He explained everything very well. Brittany was also very great, she always answered any questions I had. Also very nice and kind. I will be contacting you all in the future to for an expungement."

Lauren

First, the most common term, DUI: the act of operating a vehicle while being over the legal limit for blood alcohol content (BAC). In Oklahoma, a BAC of .08 percent or higher constitutes DUI for any driver 21 years of age or older. In Oklahoma, a BAC of .04 percent or higher constitutes a DUI for commercial driver's license, which can amount to one drink within a relatively short period of time for some individuals. Additionally, in Oklahoma, a driver under the age of 21 can be convicted of DUI for a BAC above zero percent.

DUI does not only apply to motor vehicles, cars. It can apply to boats, utility vehicles, all-terrain vehicles (ATV), motorcycles, mopeds, heavy machinery/construction equipment, and other conveyances. Additionally, DUI can be constituted by drugs, commonly referred to as DUI-D.

Second, APC: the act of being in physical control of a motor vehicle or other conveyance, discussed above, while under the influence of alcohol/drugs. You can be arrested, charged, and convicted of APC for being asleep in a parked car while intoxicated, if you are on or adjacent to a public road. However, there are detailed elements, which the prosecution must present in order to obtain a conviction for the charge of APC. It is essential your attorney know and hold the prosecution to these requirements.

Implied Consent in Oklahoma: as mentioned earlier, driving is a privilege, not a right; therefore, all drivers implicitly consent to one of the following tests to determine if a driver is intoxicated. Blood test, to determine chemical makeup of your blood, i.e. BAC: Urinalysis to determine BAC: or, a breath test i.e., Breathalyzer to determine the alcohol content of your breath, to formulate a BAC.

Failure to submit to one of the Oklahoma tests can subject you to harsh penalties related to your driver's license privilege, as well as criminal and financial penalties.

Consequences of A DUI Conviction in Oklahoma

A criminal charge and a warrant for arrest, in District or Municipal Court, will follow an arrest for DUI, DWI, or APC. Being convicted of one of these offenses comes with harsh penalties, including, but not limited to the following:

- Loss of your Driver's License or Commercial Driver's License privileges
- Mandatory completion of an alcohol/drug assessment and program (ADSAC)
- Attendance of a Victim's Impact Panel
- Narcotics Anonymous (NA) or Alcoholics Anonymous (AA) meetings
- Jail-time. Including potentially weekends in jail
- Community Service hours
- Ignition control device, installed in any vehicle you operate at your expense
- Personal and professional consequences

Know Your Options, if Charged with a DUI Crime in Oklahoma

It is important to know your rights and retain an Oklahoma criminal defense attorney with experience defending DUI; DWI; and APC cases as soon as possible. Your life and freedom are on the line, and you need a defense. Defenses are available in your criminal case and administrative proceeding before DPS, but you need a defense attorney who can use this information to your benefit.

The fact you were arrested and charged with DUI does not mean you will be convicted. You have rights and your attorney will ensure they are protected. Defenses are available to contest your charges and the tests police conducted; however, an experienced DUI defense attorney is needed to maximize your chance for a successful outcome.

An experienced Oklahoma DUI attorney can reduce the negative impact your case has on your life and may be able to obtain a dismissal. The following are common Constitutional and other legal grounds to be raised by your Oklahoma DUI defense attorney that may result in dismissal of all charges:

- Police lacked probable cause to pull you over, a Constitutional requirement prior to seizing a driver;
- Police violated your right to access to counsel;
- Improper questioning by police;
- Improper search of your vehicle or person.
- The testing device, Breathalyzer or BAC device, was not functioning correctly or not calibrated correctly.
- You were not legally in "actual physical control" of a vehicle.

You can learn more about the legal aspects of DUI traffic stops and jurisdiction by visiting our website for hundreds of resources on DUI defense.

Unfortunately, facing a DUI charge is a very common problem for people in Oklahoma. However, with an experienced defense team that uses procedures to identify the best course of action for every client and an understanding of this complex area of the law, your rights can be protected, and you can seek to protect your driving privileges.

DUI IMPACT ON DRIVING PRIVILEGE

"I highly recommend Cannon & Associates to anyone in need of an attorney for any reason. If they are unable to take your case they assist you in finding someone who can. I want to personally thank Kelly Byrd for her quick response in helping me and my family get the attorney we needed and the continued contact to make sure we were doing well. That true care for people is hard to find in attorneys and this law firm absolutely cares ▢ ▢THANK YOU SO VERY MUCH!!"

Ashlee

The Court has routinely held that driving is a privilege, not a right. Therefore, given the correct circumstance, the privilege can be suspended, revoked, or modified. The Oklahoma legislature has put multiple laws in place that dictate the impact on your driving privileges after a DUI and any other moving violation related to a motor vehicle and alcohol.

As an extension of driving being a privilege, certain rights are forfeited by law, when you elect to drive on public roads. One of the most important rights forfeited is the warrant requirement for search and seizure of the blood alcohol content of any driver. Meaning, Oklahoma law presumes every driver gives implied consent to have his or her breath tested for blood alcohol content ("BAC") when they chose to drive on public roadways in Oklahoma. The statute authorizing is Oklahoma Statutes Title 47, Section 751, which states:

> "Any person who operates a motor vehicle upon the public roads... within this state shall be deemed to have given consent to a test or tests of such person's blood or breath, for the purpose of determining the alcohol concentration."

OKLA. STAT. tit. 47 § 751(A)(1)

The Oklahoma Department of Public Safety (DPS) is the government agency that governs driving privileges for all driver's licenses in the State of Oklahoma. However, that agency operates under the laws passed by the Legislature. Until November 2019, the Erin Sweezey Act governed Driver's License proceedings through DPS, which provided more due process, or hearing rights, than what exists today.

End of Erin Swezey Act

November 1, 2019, a massive substantive and procedural change went into law removing the Erin Swezey Act and creating the Impaired Driver Accountability Program (IDAP). The new law changed how driver's license revocations and suspension proceedings are handled across the state. The new law removed due process hearing rights that existed under the previous Erin Swezey Act and changed the governance of driver's license privileges and revocations.

The IDAP laws removed Implied Consent Hearings, an important due process right related to the statute quoted above, and instituted a broader diversion program without any internal hearing process. Prior to the new law, you were entitled to an Implied Consent Hearing before a hearing officer at DPS, to determine the validity of the traffic stop, field sobriety tests, and subsequent state test for BAC related to your DUI or APC arrest in Oklahoma. If you were unsuccessful in the administrative hearing, you could file a District Court Appeal ("DCA"), to seek judicial reconsideration of the DPS hearing officer's decision.

Under the new law, Oklahoma Senate Bill 712 (SB 712) the administrative hearing was removed, and you must immediately file a "District Court Appeal" or petition in District Court, if you decline to immediately participate in the new Impaired Driver Accountability Program (IDAP) through DPS.

Can I Keep My Driver's License after a DUI?

Unfortunately, the answer is it depends. The process for restoring complete driving privileges in Oklahoma is based on the option you choose after DPS initiates an action on your Driver's License. Now that SB 712 is in effect; drivers in Oklahoma have three options related to seeking to keep their drive driving privileges:

1. **Apply for the Impaired Driver Accountability Program ("IDAP");**
2. **File District Court Appeal ("DCA") to contest the traffic stop, field sobriety tests, or the chemical test;**
3. **Do Nothing – consequences of this choice are explained below.**

In the IDAP program, drivers receive incentives to complete the program. The ignition interlock device requirement from the Erin Swezey Act is still in effect. However, the length of time the device is required in your vehicle is reduced and the previous harsh punishment for drivers with a blood-alcohol content ("BAC") of .15 or higher is gone.

Upon successful completion of IDAP, or if you prevail on your District Court Appeal, your driver's license privileges will be restored/remain in effect. However, if you fail IDAP, do not enroll in IDAP, lose your DCA, or do nothing, then your license will be revoked.

What If I Challenge The DUI Stop Or Administration Of The Breath/Blood Test?

As mentioned above, you still have a right to challenge the DUI traffic stop, testing, and/or arrest. However, the Administrative

Hearing phase is now gone. Meaning, you must immediately file a case in District Court, which is called a District Court Appeal ("DCA"). The DCA is an appeal of DPS' administrative action against your driving privileges.

The following are important facts and rules to remember in relation to filing and processing a DCA.

- District Court Appeal: it must be filed properly by you or your DUI defense attorney in the right district within thirty (30) days of your Notice of Revocation.
- District Court Hearing: you must set the hearing with the Court 15-30 days after the petition is filed;
- Court Clerk: you must ensure the Court Clerk sends a certified copy of the Petition and Order for Hearing to DPS;
- Cash Bond: it has been terminated following the Erin Swezey Act being repealed. Previously, in order to initiate a District Court Appeal you were required to post a $250 bond;
- License During Appeal: statutes do not answer whether your license is revoked pending your DCA; however, DPS' policy is to issue a stay of the revocation pending DCA;

During the hearing you or your DUI defense attorney will question officers/witnesses and present argument to the judge. Your driving privileges will remain in effect if you win; however, if you lose the hearing your license will be revoked by DPS, unless you appeal to the Oklahoma Supreme Court. You can request the Court to Order DPS to issue a modified license, if you lose your District Court Appeal and the Court has the authority to do so. You will be required to install an interlock device, if granted a modified license by DPS.

How Does District Court Decide the Appeal?

At the actual DCA hearing, the Court will hear evidence and testimony, including from the arresting officer in your DUI. The

Court must determine if reasonable grounds exist to believe you were operating a motor vehicle while intoxicated or in actual physical control of a motor vehicle, while intoxicated. Additionally, the Court will consider the validity of your arrest.

The Court applies the preponderance of the evidence burden in evaluating whether or not law enforcement complied with the requirements of the implied consent statute. You must convince the Court that your rights were violated or DPS will win the hearing.

As mentioned in the previous section, you can request the Court enter an Order for a modified license, if you are unsuccessful in the DCA hearing. Alternatively, you may also appeal the Court's decision to the Oklahoma Supreme Court, if you are not satisfied with the outcome and believe the Court was incorrect in applying the law. This process is best executed with the assistance of an experienced DUI defense attorney.

What About Appeals on Breath/Blood Tests?

District Court Appeals involving a Breath test or Blood test to determine Blood-Alcohol Content will address the legal requirements for when testing occurs and the proper procedure and calibration of the testing equipment. The following are the most common arguments at DCA regarding testing:

1. Timeliness: you were denied a timely requested breath or blood test
1. Two-hour timeframe: the breath or blood specimen was not obtained within two hours of arrest
2. Under 21: failure of the officer to notify you that your driving privileges will be revoked or suspended, if the test reflects any quantity of alcohol, i.e. 0.02 BAC, is a defense
3. Over 21: failure of the officer to advise you that your driving privileges would be revoked or suspended, if the test result reflects a BAC at or above 0.08 BAC.
4. Test: The test result must in fact reflect the alcohol concentration.

5. Refusals: appeals involving alleged refusal to submit to testing revolve around the defense that the driver did not refuse to submit to the state's test and the driver was not notified of the consequences of failing to submit to testing.

What is the Impaired Driver Accountability Program?

The Impaired Driver Accountability Program ("IDAP") is a "voluntary" program within the Department of Public Safety. Its purpose is to encourage driver's with a DUI or APC to install an ignition interlock device in their vehicle. Drivers must apply to participate in IDAP. Upon DPS accepting you into the IDAP program; you must enroll in the program and complete the initiation requirements within 30 days of enrollment.

There are many benefits to IDAP that you should consider. First and foremost, your license will not be revoked or suspended for participating. You will not have to pay a reinstatement fee after completing IDAP. Upon IDAP completion, you can go to any Tag Agency and get a new driver's license. Your ignition interlock period can run concurrently or at the same time as a court order in your criminal case for DUI or APC, i.e. no double punishment of an interlock twice, if your defense attorney is able to get the criminal case interlock time-line to run concurrently with IDAP. Your DUI or APC will not appear on DPS record searches; however, it can enhance, if you have a second or subsequent offense.

How to Apply to IDAP?

Not every driver is eligible for IDAP. You can only apply for IDAP, if you are a non-commercial driver, i.e. hold a Class D driver's license. All Commercial Drivers, CDL holders, must file the District Court Appeal discussed above to save their commercial driver's license from being revoked, or voluntarily surrender your CDL and downgrade to a Class D, non-commercial driver's license.

You are entitled to notice of IDAP from the arresting officer in your DUI offense. Similar to the DCA process, you only have thirty (30) days to apply to IDAP from notice of revocation. However, DPS has the authority to approve late applications. It is best to consult a DUI defense attorney and submit your late request for IDAP admission through counsel, if you are past the 30-day time frame to apply to IDAP.

You or your DUI defense attorney must submit your IDAP application to DPS by one of the three following means within 30 days: mail your application to DPS headquarters, email it to **IDAP@dps.gov**, or hand deliver it to DPS. We recommend emailing and mailing your application and maintaining a record proving mailing. The date you mail, postmark date, is considered the date you applied for IDAP.

Additionally, you can request IDAP from a hearing officer at DPS. DPS currently issues a stay on revoking your driver's license until sixteen days after the IDAP request deadline in your case, which means you have 45 days to apply and complete enrollment in IDAP after your notice of revocation.

When it comes to DPS and IDAP, silence is the same as rejecting the program. When or if you fail to complete the IDAP application process timely, DPS actions your license as if you rejected the offer for IDAP participation. These complex issues are best understood with the assistance of an experienced DUI defense attorney.

Completing Enrollment in IDAP

As stated above, it is not sufficient to merely submit your application for IDAP to DPS. **You must complete IDAP enrollment and all the following steps in order to be admitted and participate in the program:**

- Complete IDAP Participant Agreement Form, which must be signed by DPS Hearing Officer. Pay $200 to DPS, and $50 for a restricted driver's license during IDAP participation.
- Only drive a vehicle with ignition interlock device, unless employer exception to requirement applies;

- Provide DPS proof of instillation of an ignition interlock device, which must be within 45 days of the notice. Again, DPS has authority to grant exceptions to this requirement;
- Acknowledge receipt and review of IDAP Participant Guide;

Additional important notes on IDAP enrollment:

- *IDAP for subsequent DUI/APC convictions are completed consecutively;*
- *Program requirements and restrictions apply through the last day of IDAP;*
- *You must COMPLETE IDAP before removing the ignition interlock.*

How is my date of Notice of Revocation determined?

The date of Notice of Revocation of your driving privileges subsequent to a DUI or APC arrest in Oklahoma is based on the test administered following your DUI. The date of Notice of Revocation is the date you were arrested, if you took a breath test or refused the same.

In cases involving a blood test, the date of your Notice of Revocation is ten days after DPS mails you or your defense counsel. It is wise to assume the earliest date, i.e. the date of your DUI or APC and work with an experienced DUI defense attorney immediately to initiate your DCA, get enrolled in IDAP, or both.

What is an Ignition Interlock Device?

The ignition interlock device, or 'breath alcohol ignition interlock device' is a Breathalyzer for your personal vehicle. The driver is required to blow into a mouthpiece on the device before the engine will start in the vehicle. When or if the blood alcohol content detected is higher than the device's program limitation, the vehicle will not start. The device is connected directly to the vehicle's ignition system for the engine. These devices are a type of electronic monitoring system, which interrupts the ignition's signal from reaching the vehicle's starter, until a breath sample is provided that is below the legal limit.

How Do I Obtain an Ignition Interlock Device?

You must obtain an ignition interlock device from a provider registered by the Oklahoma Board of Tests. There are many providers; however, only a handful are approved for use by the Oklahoma Department of Public Safety. Your interlock device will not be accepted if it is not installed by an approved vendor within the State of Oklahoma.

The following page has a list of every approved Ignition Interlock provider in Oklahoma at the time of this writing:

https://pay.apps.ok.gov/bot/ignition/app/list_manufacturers.php

How Long Do I Have To Keep An Interlock In My Car Under IDAP?

The length of time that the ignition interlock device is required on your vehicle is determined by your history with DPS and whether or not your license has previously been suspended for DUI. The minimum time an interlock must be installed in your vehicle is as follows based on your number of offenses:

First Offense: Six (6) Months

Second Offense: Twelve (12) Months

Third Offense: Thirty-Six (36) Months

Note that there is no more "extra interlock time" pursuant to the Erin Swezey Act. Once you complete IDAP, you can drive with a normal license and without an interlock–regardless of whether you refused or how many times you've been arrested for DUI. However, many prosecution offices require you install an ignition interlock device on your vehicle as part of probation as well. It is important to work with your DUI defense attorney to ensure you comply in all aspects of your case.

What is an Interlock Violation?

An interlock violation is the occurrence of an event that is prohibited by the ignition interlock requirements. When one of the following events occurs, it is required that your ignition interlock provider reports the violations at certain points.

- Three penalty fails at startup within a 15-minute timeframe
- Three retest violations constitutes a reportable violation.
- Circumvention of the interlock device
- Unauthorized removal of the interlock device, except:
- Upon receipt of documentation from the installation authority or monitor authorizing that removal
- The vehicle is being repaired. In this situation, the program participant must inform the licensed service center at least every eight days as to the anticipated date of completion of repairs; or
- The vehicle is being replaced. If your vehicle is being replaced with another vehicle, then the removal and reinstallation of the device in the new vehicle has to be accomplished within eight days of the removal of the device from the old vehicle;
- Tampering with the device or missing a service appointment

What Happens if an Interlock violation occurs in IDAP?

Each retest violation after the first three constitutes a reportable violation. During Phase I of the IDAP program, the length of program cannot be extended for a violation. However, DPS has the authority to take measures to correct misconduct or violations, including removal from the program, which would result in the revocation of your driving privileges.

Alternatively, DPS may require instillation of a device with a camera, or restriction on days and times you may drive, which can cause serious problems in other areas of your life.

There's a period of time in which an IDAP participant is subject to program extension due to interlock violations or program violations.

Six-month period: The program will be extended for 60 days, if you commit a violation during the last 60 days of the original program.

One-year period: The program will be extended 120 days, if you commit a violation during the last 120 days of the original program.

Three-year period: The program will be extended one (1) year / 365 days, if you commit a violation during the last year of the original program.

What Can DPS do if I Have a Verified Interlock Violation during IDAP?

DPS may impose any of the following punishments or sanctions, if you commit a violation during IDAP:

- Retraining with manufacturer, at the expense of the participant;
- Installation of an interlock with a camera
- Restrictions on the days and times of the participant's driving;
- Referral to re-assessment; and
- Removal from IDAP, which will result in a driver license revocation.

You may appear before a DPS Hearing Officer within 15 days of receipt of the notice of violation to contest that violation. The Hearing Officer may sustain or set aside the violation. If you don't contest the violation within those 15 days, then you have waived any future right to contest that violation.

How Do I Graduate from IDAP?

In order to graduate from IDAP, you must give the following to DPS:

- IDAP Completion Form, which is obtained from the Board of Tests. The IDAP Completion Form verifies no interlock violations occurred during the last 60, 120, or 365 days of the program;
- Drug and Alcohol Assessment ("ADSAC") Completion Certificate; and
- No DUI arrests during IDAP participation. DPS verifies this by checking for Officer Affidavits and Notices of Revocation;

Upon successful completion, DPS will update your Driver Index to reflect the completion of IDAP and issue you a Certificate. Additionally, upon successful completion of IDAP, no revocation will appear upon your driving record.

What Happens if I do nothing within 30 Days?

Your license may be revoked, if you do nothing within 30 days of notice of revocation, i.e. your arrest for DUI. If the notice of revocation is not provided to DPS timely, you may be able to submit a late application to IDAP; however, DPS has discretion to deny your late application. Therefore it is crucial you or your DUI defense attorney not hesitate, and you initiate one of the following within 30 days of your notice of revocation:

- Challenge your DUI arrest through a District Court Action;
- Apply to the IDAP within 30 days of your arrest or Notice of Revocation, if you were administered a blood test after your DUI.

Your driver's license will be revoked 30 days after your DUI/APC arrest or Notice or Revocation, if you fail to take one of these actions, once DPS learns of your notice of revocation.

One wrinkle is your revocation will go into effect 40 days after being mailed a Notice of Revocation following the results of a blood test, determining your BAC after a DUI.

DPS must issue you a Modified License upon request. An interlock device must be installed on your vehicle for the entire modification period; however, DPS may modify this time to twelve (12) months. The time periods are the same if you lose your District Court Appeal or District Court Action (Contesting the DUI stop, DUI/Field Sobriety Tests, or blood test).

Will my Driver's License Revocation run with my Ignition Interlock?

Yes, your driver's license revocation/suspension and ignition interlock periods can run together. However, if you and your DUI defense lawyer cannot get the start dates to match; then you will have a period without overlap, i.e. you will have the interlock device on your vehicle longer than six months, if your modified license period does not start with your probation period in your Oklahoma DUI case. One of the best things your DUI defense attorney can do for you, other than being Your Fierce Advocates® is to have both interlock periods run together.

Will I lose my Driver's License, If I lose in District Court?

Yes, your license will be revoked/suspended, if you lose your District Court Action against DPS. However, SB 712 did not change the time requirements for the interlock device after a DUI offense:

*** With the Erin Swezey Act going away; there is no extra interlock time following revocation. Once you are reinstated you can drive without an interlock; regardless of refusing the state's test or your number of DUI offenses.

What if I Get another DUI during my Driver's License Revocation?

First, you should immediately seek the assistance of an experienced Oklahoma DUI Defense Lawyer. However, a second DUI during your revocation will result in an extended period of driver's license modification, unless your license is revoked. And, you will face a second, separate, criminal charge.

Another issue is you cannot have a violation within 180 days or six (6) months of your release from a modified license. Which means, if you are on a six (6) month modified license and have a violation on the last day, you will have to start the six (6) month period over.

Can I fight my Driver's License Case and Apply to IDAP?

Yes and No. You may both apply to IDAP and file a District Court Appeal (DCA); however, you only have 45 days from the notice of revocation to get into compliance and complete your registration with IDAP. Therefore, you may initiate the process for both; however, you will be required to dismiss your DCA appeal prior to 45 days after your notice of revocation, in order to be allowed to participate in IDAP.

Unless you contact and hire an experienced DUI Defense attorney immediately after your DUI stop; you will likely not have sufficient time to obtain the reports and/or dash cam footage of your DUI traffic stop to help decide whether or not you want to challenge the stop in District Court. Therefore, most drivers will have to decide without potentially available information, if they want to challenge the DUI stop or tests through a District Court Appeal or submit to participation in IDAP.

What if I was Arrested before the Law Changed?

The date of Revocation, not the DUI arrest date, determines the law that will apply to your case. The Erin Swezey Act will apply to revocations prior to November 1, 2019, which means potential additional interlock time. However, if your revocation occurred on or after November 1, 2019 then the Erin Swezey Act does not apply and you will not be subject to additional ignition interlock time, i.e. after IDAP completion.

This rule applies regardless of what action you take in your driver's license case with DPS: request an administrative hearing, stay the revocation, take no action, or take District Court Appeal action.

What is the Excessive User Program?

The Excessive User Program no longer exists after SB 712 passed. However, it does not apply retroactively; meaning you will have to abide by the Excessive User Program requirements, if you were designated as an Excessive User prior to November 1, 2019. Oklahoma drivers will not have to abide by Excessive User requirements unless a revocation is in place and final prior to November 1, 2019.

Why are Ignition Interlock Devices still used?

Ignition Interlock Devices ("IID") are still relevant, because research shows they are the most effective tool or way to reduce drunk driving. Oklahoma's new laws make the process of reinstatement of driving privileges simpler. However, the right to an Administrative Hearing and the inability to challenge your DUI stop and participate in IDAP at the same time leaves challenges for law makers and DUI Defense Lawyers to address.

Your Driver's License after DUI in Oklahoma

The process for recovering your Driver's License or seeking a Modified Driver's License is a complex process with very particular procedures. It is crucial you contact an experienced criminal defense attorney, if you are facing a DUI or the potential to have your license revoked by the Oklahoma Department of Public Safety (DPS).

If you think the process and legal issues involved with DPS are complicated, you are correct. The process of seeking to protect your driver's license after a DUI or APC is highly technical and all errors are held against you, not the state. It is important you hire an experienced DUI defense attorney that understands DPS legal procedures and can hold the state to its procedural and legal burdens. Your driver's license is too important to let chance control the outcome.

DO FIRST TIME DUI OFFENDERS GO TO JAIL?

"Recently called Cannon & Associates seeking legal advice. All of my questions were well received and answered very knowledgeably by Kelly. The office is beautiful, everyone is very respect and courteous, as well as extremely knowledgeable and professional. I would highly recommend this law firm to anyone facing a DUI or any legal situation."

Kasey

Unfortunately, the answer is it depends.

Drunk driving is a crime across the United States. While state laws may differ, the consequences of a DUI are similar in most states. A DUI case becomes more serious when the life of uninvolved motorists are put in jeopardy or, even worse, if an injury accident or death results from drunk driving. Oklahoma DUI offenses come in a number of shapes and sizes, ranging from first-time misdemeanor DUI offenses to felony DUI or vehicular homicides related to a DUI accident.

After a DUI arrest in made in Oklahoma, it is common for criminal defendants to sober up, and along with this comes a ton of questions including what their fate will be in the coming days. One of the toughest pills to swallow is an Oklahoma DUI conviction and so, naturally, the question of whether you will have to serve jail time comes to mind.

It is important to note all DUI convictions, whether a first-time offense or subsequent offenses, carry the possibility of jail time as part of its penalty. The difference, however, is in the length of the jail sentence.

For example, a first felony DUI conviction in Oklahoma can carry between 1 to 5 years of prison, while a second and subsequent felony DUI offenders can expect between 1 to 10 years of prison time. Third or more felony DUI offenses within a ten-year period carries 1 to 20 years in prison.

Although the possibility of avoiding jail on a felony DUI may appear low, there are steps you can take to reduce the chance of jail or prison time on any Oklahoma DUI offense.

Avoiding Jail on DUI Arrest

While hiring an Oklahoma DUI attorney is a great start towards achieving the goal of escaping jail, you must know that the outcome of your defense is in the hands of the judge. The chances an Oklahoma DUI convict, especially a first-time offender, will spend time in jail depends on the final ruling of the judge presiding over the case. However, working with an experienced Oklahoma DUI attorney can open up multiple options or outcomes to help you avoid jail time.

Your Oklahoma DUI defense lawyer can explore all of the legal options available towards achieving the goal, but the decision of the judge is final. If the judge considers the defendant's counsel and his or her argument against jail term, then an alternative sentence may be issued. Several alternative outcomes can be considered in place of jail time, and many of these consequences can be avoided by Fierce Advocacy and a resolution with the prosecutor on your DUI case.

Some of the alternatives to jail time on an Oklahoma DUI case, include:

DUI Probation

DUI Probation is an alternative that gives you the opportunity to avoid any jail time on your DUI offense, if you are successful on probation. If your Oklahoma City DUI lawyer has been able to prove to the prosecutor and the judge that you are remorseful for your actions and will refrain from further DUI offenses, the judge and prosecutor may agree to order probation in place of jail time.

During your DUI probation period, you will be released from police custody and will have the freedom to go about your life; however, you will be under the supervision of a probation officer who will decide whether you are following the specific rules that have been laid out for the duration of the probation.

The typical terms of probation on a DUI offense include some or all of the following:

- Complete Drug and Alcohol Assessment and follow the recommendations
- Victim Impact Panel
- Attendance of AA or NA Meetings
- In-Patient or Out-Patient services
- Community Service
- Interlock Device be installed on your vehicle, if you are allowed to drive
- Restitution, if you caused damage, i.e. a DUI involving an accident
- Court Costs and Fines
- Obtain from consuming alcohol or illegal drugs

The benefits of probation may be removed, if you fail to comply with the conditions of your probation. When the prosecutor or probation office allege to the Court that you have violated the conditions of your DUI probation, a hearing will be set and the Court will decide to take away / revoke your DUI probation or allow you to remain on DUI probation. An experienced Oklahoma DUI defense attorney can assist you in avoiding this negative outcome; again however, the final decision is in the judge's hands on your Oklahoma DUI.

DUI House Arrest

One alternative to jail time that is more serious than probation is DUI house arrest. If ordered to DUI house arrest you will be required to confine yourself within your residence and wear a GPS ankle monitor to ensure you remain in your home for the duration of your DUI house arrest probation.

Community Service for DUI

DUI probation often includes the requirement to compete community service hours. You may be presented with a wide variety of options, if you are required to complete community service, which may include manual labor or office work. An experienced Oklahoma City DUI attorney can assist you in seeking to reduce your DUI community service obligation and also make it more manageable with your school or work schedule.

Alcohol or Drug Rehabilitation following a DUI

Many patient services exist to help address issues that may lead to a DUI arrest. These alternatives include in-patient and out-patient treatment options to help you avoid a conviction and/or jail time. The duration of these programs can differ widely; however, with the assistance of an experienced Oklahoma City DUI attorney, you may be able to identify and complete a program prior to resolution of your Oklahoma City DUI offense.

Completing any DUI treatment or alcohol treatment, especially in-patient or out-patient, prior to the resolution of your Oklahoma DUI offense will increase the chance of your Oklahoma City DUI attorney being able to reach the best outcome possible for your DUI case. Treatment options for a DUI or alcohol related offense may be difficult; however, these options are far better than jail or prison time.

DUI Court

Many district courts in Oklahoma offer DUI Court or DUI/Drug Court as an alternative to jail or prison time on a DUI offense. These programs involve supervised probation and appearances before the DUI Court judge to ensure you are complying with the requirements of the DUI Court program. Although more intensive than DUI probation, these programs offer an opportunity to remain out of jail or out of custody in exchange for compliance with the DUI Court program. Your chosen DUI defense attorney should explore these options on your behalf, if you have a history of DUI offenses or are charged with a felony DUI in Oklahoma.

Victim Impact Program

Victim Impact Panel is a statewide requirement for DUI offenses, which is an initiative from Mothers Against Drunk Driving (MADD). The Victim Impact Panel (VIP) is an in person or online seminar that DUI offenders are required to complete upon admission into any DUI probation program. However, our DUI defense attorneys recommend completion of this program and other conditions of probation prior to sentencing as the court, and prosecutors look very favorably on DUI defendants that complete terms of probation before resolving a DUI case.

During the Victim Impact Panel, you will hear from speakers that are victims of DUI accidents as well as survivors and family of loved ones that experienced serious injury or fatality in DUI accidents. These meetings last roughly 3 hours and are desired as a "scared straight approach" to DUI offenders.

CRIMINAL CHARGES FOR YOUTH IN OKLAHOMA

"I've worked with Jennifer in the past. It's great to see her working with Cannon & Associates. Her heart and passion has always been to help the community any way she can. With Jennifer, I guarantee you'll be treated with kindness and compassion!"

Sara

Our justice system is focused on rehabilitation of minors in the juvenile justice system. However, what prosecutors and judges define as "rehabilitation" is an area of great concern for families with children facing the justice system.

Defending children and minors presents many unique challenges that do not exist in adult criminal procedure. The process for criminal proceedings involving children can change in an instant, based on a number of factors. Some of the factors influencing the course of a criminal case for a minor can be impacted by the defendant and his or her criminal defense attorney. However, many of the factors that determine the specific process you will face are outside of the parties' control.

Juvenile Criminal Defense

Children and teenagers facing the difficulties of life, school, family, and peer pressure sometimes turn to poor outlets and choices, including drugs, alcohol, and crime. Cannon & Associates works every day to ensure our clients' bad choices, or false accusations, don't ruin their lives.

When faced with these circumstances, families need quality and compassionate defense counsel with experience defending juvenile criminal cases. Based in part on the complexity of the criminal process involved in these cases, it is critical you choose the right juvenile criminal defense attorney to protect your future and your rights during the case. The stakes when a minor child is accused or charged with a crime are very high. A conviction for a violent or serious offense can have consequences that follow someone into adulthood.

Juvenile criminal prosecution is more similar to family law than adults criminal cases in some respects. There are multiple different processes that occur at the same time, focusing on the case at hand as well as the minor, independent of the criminal case. The most important determination is how the minor will be charged and tried as 1) a delinquent, 2) youthful offender, or 3) adult.

Children facing criminal charges in Oklahoma are subject to one of the three proceedings under the Oklahoma Youthful Offender Act, which begins at Oklahoma Statutes Title 10A, Sections 2-5-201:

1. Juvenile Delinquent

2. Youthful Offender

3. An Adult

Each category has a different purpose and procedures, which an experienced juvenile criminal defense attorney will ensure are respected for the benefit of your case.

One of the most important processes in this area is the Certification Hearing. The outcome of this hearing determines the most important question; will your case be handled as an adult or as a minor?

Juvenile Delinquent Adjudication

In Oklahoma, minors under the age of eighteen are not convicted for crimes, unless charged and convicted with specific offenses, discussed below. A child or teen with a juvenile delinquent adjudication may spend time in a detention facility, but the records will be sealed and not visible to the public.

This is the least serious of the three categories of processes, and is generally reserved for minor offenses by children fifteen years old or younger. When a minor's case is handled as a juvenile delinquent, it increases the likelihood of no consequences following the minor to adulthood.

Youthful Offenders

Youthful offender classification is far more serious than juvenile delinquent proceedings; however, it is still not adult prosecution. The youthful offender proceedings should not be taken lightly, as a potential consequence is certification and prosecution as an adult.

All youthful offender cases in Oklahoma are prosecuted under the Oklahoma Youthful Offender Act, Oklahoma Statutes Title 10A beginning at Section 2-5-201. The youthful offender act is reserved for serious criminal offenses, as it may expose children to adult prosecution, which goes against the presumption that juvenile prosecution should not follow a minor's record into adulthood.

When the youthful offender process goes well for your loved one he or she may be released without further prosecution. However, if it goes poorly, your loved one may be prosecuted and sentenced as an adult. Juvenile cases have specific time and pleading requirements, which your attorney must meet in order to protect your rights or the rights of a child facing this process.

Additionally, experienced juvenile criminal defense counsel can seek relief, including dismissal of the case, if the prosecutor fails to follow the Youthful Offender process. Juvenile criminal defense counsel must seek certification as a juvenile, and certification as a Youthful Offender, by filing the proper paperwork by the required timeline. Failure to do so may waive your right to these proceedings.

Being sentenced as a Youthful Offender is not a conviction in the typical sense, unless the child is bridged to custody of, or supervision by, the Department of Corrections. The purpose of these proceedings is two-fold:

- protect the public from the most serious juvenile offenders; and
- Rehabilitate youths through the Office of Juvenile Affairs

What Crimes fall under Youthful Offender?

In order to face youthful offender prosecution, you must be charged with an enumerated youthful offender offense. These offenses are limited to the most serious crimes. Additionally, in order to face youthful offender prosecution, a teen must be between the age of fifteen and seventeen, when charged with the specific crime. The following offenses are the limits of the youthful offender crimes list:

- Second Degree Murder
- First Degree Manslaughter
- Shooting with Intent to Kill
- Discharging a Weapon from a Vehicle
- Aggravated Assault and Battery on an Officer
- Assault and Battery with a Deadly Weapon
- Maiming
- Witness Intimidation
- Assault
- Kidnapping
- Armed Robbery / Attempted Armed Robbery
- First Degree Rape / Attempted First Degree Rape
- Rape & Attempted Rape by Instrumentation
- Second Degree Rape
- Forcible Sodomy
- Lewd Molestation
- First Degree Arson / Attempted First Degree Arson
- First Degree Burglary / Attempted First Degree Burglary
- Second Degree Burglary, after two or more adjudications

- Drug Trafficking
- Drug Manufacturing

When Are Minors Charged as Adults?

Only in the most serious circumstances will a minor be charged as an adult, without first facing the youthful offender process, principally Murder in the First Degree. In all cases that qualify under the Youthful Offender Statute, the Court must consider a number of guidelines in determining whether a child will be tried as an adult or not.

The following factors are considered by the Court in determining whether a youthful offender will be certified as an adult or remain a juvenile. Therefore, it is important to remember that the arguments your criminal defense attorney presents to support certification as a juvenile may decide the course of the case. The Court is required to give the first three (3) factors great weight; however, all the factors are taken into consideration:

Whether the alleged offense was committed in an aggressive, violent, premeditated or willful manner;

Whether the offense was against persons and, if personal injury resulted, the degree of personal injury;

The record and past history of the accused person, including previous contacts with law enforcement agencies and juvenile or criminal courts, prior periods of probation and commitments to juvenile institutions;

The sophistication and maturity of the accused person and the accused person's capability of distinguishing right from wrong, as determined by consideration of the accused person's psychological evaluation, home, environmental situation, emotional attitude and pattern of living;

The prospects for adequate protection of the public if the accused person is processed through the youthful offender system or the juvenile system;

The reasonable likelihood of rehabilitation of the accused person if the accused is found to have committed the alleged offense, by the use of procedures and facilities currently available to the juvenile court; and

Whether the offense occurred while the accused person was escaping or in an escape status from an institution for youthful offenders or juvenile delinquents.

See OKLA. STAT. tit. 10A, Sections 2-5-206(F)(4)

You or your loved ones are entitled to a defense, and you need a Fierce Advocate®, if you are facing a juvenile or youthful offender charge in Oklahoma. Cannon & Associates can assist you and ensure your rights are protected. The system can appear biased against an accused child, hiring the right defense firm will ensure your or your child's rights are respected from initial investigation through sentencing.

Our team of criminal defense attorneys at Cannon & Associates have represented many families facing the Oklahoma juvenile justice system. We would be glad to meet with you, discuss your options, and answer all your questions about the road ahead.

SECTION FOUR: FEDERAL CRIMINAL DEFENSE

FEDERAL CRIMINAL DEFENSE

"Flat out one of the most professional attorneys that I have had the pleasure of meeting. He loves his work, loves helping people and if clearly shows. I highly recommend him and his team of Fierce Advocates."

Alton

FEDERAL INVESTIGATIONS

The federal government has more resources and more specific purposes of investigating alleged crimes than state and local agencies. Therefore, federal investigations are often more thorough and conducted with greater resources than state court investigations. This chapter discusses an overview of federal investigations and their implications.

How Are Federal Investigations Conducted?

Multiple federal agencies have criminal investigative units, or divisions, that collect and provide investigations to the United States Attorney's Office in the Federal District in which the events occurred. Despite the common perspective, that the Federal Bureau of Investigation (FBI), the Drug Enforcement Administration (DEA), and Bureau of Alcohol, Tobacco, Firearms and Explosions (ATF) conduct all federal criminal investigations, most federal agencies have a federal criminal investigative unit. However, the majority of federal criminal investigations are indeed conducted by the following federal agencies:

- Federal Bureau of Investigation (FBI)
- Drug Enforcement Administration (DEA)
- Bureau of Alcohol, Tobacco, Firearms and Explosives (ATF)
- United States Secret Service (USSS)
- Homeland Security Investigations (DHS/HSI)

Federal investigators work under a similar framework as local and state law enforcement; however, their authority is based on federal regulations or statutes. They have areas of interest, such as the Internal Revenue Service (IRS), whose investigators primarily investigate tax fraud and financial crime, i.e. white collar crime.

How do Federal Investigators and State Investigators Differ?

Federal investigators differ from state investigators as they play a much closer role in prosecution than state court investigators that simply present investigations for prosecutors to evaluate. Most federal investigations consist of federal prosecutors working directly alongside federal investigations over the course of an investigation, leading up to the decision to present a case to the grand jury for indictment or not.

Federal investigators interview witnesses, collect evidence, and assist prosecutors, U.S. Attorneys, in understanding the facts of a particular case, and oftentimes United States Attorney's Offices work with multiple, separate, federal agencies in one investigation.

What is Unique to Federal Investigations?

Some state court criminal investigations consist of coordination and back and forth between District Attorneys and law enforcement over a period of time; however, generally law enforcement conducts its investigation separate from state prosecution offices.

Alternatively, in federal criminal investigations the United States Attorney's Office almost always works alongside federal criminal investigators during the course of the investigation, which facilitates Federal criminal charging decisions in United States Attorney's Offices.

What happens during a Federal Investigation?

Search warrants are often requested in the course of federal criminal investigations. You have Constitutional protections under the Fourth Amendment that require probable cause before law enforcement can search your home, your person, your car, or other property, and a neutral and detached judge must sign a search warrant prior to it being executed.

Federal arrests and searches are primarily conducted after an arrest warrant, based on probable cause, is signed or issued by a federal judge. Local and state investigators often conclude investigations with a search warrant being executed; however, the majority of state criminal cases come from arrests by local law enforcement and subsequent searches.

Federal agents do have the authority to arrest an individual at the time a crime is committed, if probable cause exists, just like state and local law enforcement; however, more often than not Federal agents act upon investigations, not simply contact with alleged suspects.

An experienced criminal defense attorney will make contact with the federal investigators in your case as well as the United States Attorney involved to advocate your position prior to a charging, indictment, or grand jury decision is reached.

What Type of Evidence is Collected in Federal Cases?

The evidence collected in the course of federal investigations is similar in form to the evidence collected in state and local law enforcement investigations; 'direct' and 'circumstantial' evidence.

Direct Evidence: the statements, photographs, video, and other information obtained during a federal investigation is reviewed and evaluated against federal law and jurisdiction by United States Attorney's Offices to determine if sufficient evidence exists to present to a Federal Grand Jury. Direct evidence supports a fact without an inference, such as eyewitness testimony, including a person's claim they actually saw a crime occur. However, testimony of something before or after an alleged crime is circumstantial evidence.

Circumstantial Evidence: all indirect information relating to a criminal act, as stated above, information before or after a crime, is circumstantial evidence. It requires an inference, or a leap from a fact known to a fact assumed.

FEDERAL COURT PROCEEDINGS OVERVIEW

"I have followed John Cannon's work and he has done great things for his clients including my loved one as the case against him was DISMISSED in FEDERAL criminal court. This is something that rarely happens as the feds have a 96% conviction rate. If you're needing representation in a criminal case you will be good in Mr. John Cannon's hands. I would like to thank Mr. Cannon and Brittany for everything because our family is now able to see the light at the end of the tunnel. I wish Cannon and Associates the best. Thank you all again!!!"

Larry

Federal prosecution is based on events that cross state lines or violate federal regulations or United States Code. Generally, state criminal proceedings cover all manner of criminal conduct, and only a limited amount and type of criminal acts are to be prosecuted or handled by the federal government; however, the size and breadth of the federal government and its interaction with citizens everyday has led to a substantial number of acts which are prosecuted or handled by federal prosecutors and federal law enforcement.

Subsequent to a criminal defendant learning they are facing indictment or federal investigation for a federal crime, he or she can hire a federal criminal defense attorney, if they have not already, or be represented by a Federal Public Defender, if they qualify as indigent. A federal criminal defense attorney is vital to understanding the federal criminal charges and the federal criminal process, including trial and sentencing.

Federal criminal cases are tried in one of the 94 Federal District Courts in the United States. Oklahoma is one of the few states that has multiple federal districts, in fact we have three: The Western District of Oklahoma (Oklahoma City), The Northern District of Oklahoma (Tulsa), and The Eastern District of Oklahoma (Muskogee). Although a federal criminal charge may be related to criminal allegations anywhere in Oklahoma, the case will be tried in one of these three federal courthouses.

Federal Criminal Charges

After federal prosecutors review the completed investigation from federal criminal investigators, they may interview witnesses or involved individuals and then make a decision to present or not present the case to the Grand Jury.

1st Step – Grand Jury

A Grand Jury, a group of impartial citizens, is called and hears the evidence against the suspect. During the grand jury, witnesses are called to testify, evidence is presented, and the federal prosecutor presents a summary of the case to the grand jury members. No indictment comes from the Grand Jury if they believe insufficient evidence exists.

The United States Constitution specifically provides the right to a Grand Jury for certain criminal offenses. The purpose, if not obvious, is to provide a criminal defendant an unbiased decision about the sufficiency of the evidence against him or her prior to being forced to face the rigor of federal prosecution.

Grand Juries consist of 16-23 members, and the proceedings cannot be viewed by anyone not specifically authorized to attend. After the Grand Jury members hear the federal prosecutor's case they vote in secret, which determines whether or not the federal criminal defendant will be charged with a crime.

All Grand Jury proceedings are sealed, which means no one except the individuals in the room know who testified, what they said, and what evidence was presented. Witnesses called to testify cannot have counsel present. At least 12 members must agree in order for an indictment to be issued.

2nd Step – Federal Indictment

Upon Indictment, the formal notice that federal prosecutor(s) believe a suspect has committed a federal crime, the suspect is notified of the federal criminal charges against him or her.

3rd Step – Arraignment

The first step after the grand jury signs an indictment is arraignment, similar to arraignment in state court criminal proceedings. At arraignment in federal court, you will enter a plea of guilty or not guilty to the charges in the indictment.

4th Step – Detention Hearing

A detention hearing will also take place immediately after a federal criminal defendant is taken into custody. During the detention hearing, the magistrate judge will make a similar evaluation of the federal criminal defendant's flight risk and threat to the community. When pretrial detention is not ordered, property may be put up as a surety; however, usually the federal criminal defendant is released without bond and ordered to appear at all court dates.

An experienced federal criminal defense attorney can assist you in obtaining release during your pending criminal case in federal court. The magistrate judge will consider a number of factors in determining whether or not the criminal defendant meets the factors for release via bail, which includes holding a hearing to determine the following factors:

- **Defendant's threat to the community;**
- **Defendant's ties to the community;**

- **Defendant's length of time in the community;**
- **Location of Defendant's family;**
- **Prior criminal record;**
- **Whether or not threats have been made to witnesses;**

At the conclusion of the hearing, the magistrate judge will determine whether or not the individual should be granted pretrial release, if not, the defendant will be remanded to the custody of the U.S. Marshal's Office until jury trial. During this time, the individual will be held at a federal facility, hopefully in close proximity to the federal court in the respective district.

When you are ordered to pretrial detention, you may appeal the determination by requesting the District Judge over your cases overrule the magistrate judge; however, it is important to make your best argument at the initial hearing.

5th Step – Scheduling Order & Accelerated Docket

The federal criminal system is more efficient and moves faster than state criminal procedures. The day, or day after, a federal criminal defendant is arrested they will be brought before a magistrate judge for their Initial Hearing, arraignment, and typically a detention hearing as well. The criminal defendant will be given a scheduling order and jury trial will be set immediately, typically within 60 to 90 days following the initial hearing.

6th Step – Discovery Process

The majority of the time and effort in a federal criminal case is after arraignment, but before federal criminal trial. Both sides will contact witnesses to learn how they will help, or more importantly, hurt, that party's case, and both sides will be providing the evidence they intend to use at trial. This process is called Discovery and is an ongoing process of discovering material, evidence, witnesses, as well as providing information to the other side.

One major issue in federal criminal defense is that many investigations include thousands of pages of reports and hours of material that must be viewed or listened to in order to digest the potential evidence for or against a client.

Although the federal prosecutor who participated in the process will be familiar with much of the evidence/case against the federal criminal defendant, a federal criminal defense attorney will not have access to this information until after arraignment.

Federal appellate courts have developed substantial case law, based on common sense, fairness, and the Constitution, which requires the government to provide evidence to the criminal defendant that may help as well as hurt their case. Evidence that may help a criminal defendant's case is called exculpatory evidence. Failure of a prosecutor, whether intentional or accidental, to provide exculpatory evidence may result in sanction, fines and, potentially, dismissal of charges or a new trial.

7th Step – Negotiation in Federal Case

The U.S. Attorney's Office is under the same time constraints as federal criminal defendants, and they often have too many cases to litigate all of them effectively. Therefore, federal prosecutors are motivated to resolve cases. An experienced federal criminal defense attorney can identify problems in the government's case that may result in an agreement to plea to lesser charges or sentencing factors that will greatly reduce your exposure during federal sentencing.

In addition to plea negotiations, federal criminal defendants may participate in a proffer, which is an opportunity to meet with federal investigators and prosecutors to potentially reduce exposure or improve the outcome of your case. The proffer meeting with federal investigators and prosecutors is an art form, which cannot be fully explained here. However, when you successfully conduct a proffer meeting, the information presented in the meeting cannot be used against you and may result in dismissal of charges or a guaranteed reduced range of punishment. It is not in your interest to conduct a proffer meeting if you plan to fight your case, as it is a slippery slop for what you can present at trial.

8th Step – Entering a Plea in Federal Court

One of the benefits of exchanging discovery, as discussed in the Discovery Process, is the development of an understanding of the strengths and weaknesses of the government's case. Meaning, the parties will exchange information and ideas concerning the case. Whether the government has a strong or weak case, it may offer to either reduce the criminal defendant's exposure to the lengthy sentences included in federal sentencing statutes, or to avoid a trial the government may or may not win.

In order to enter a plea of guilty, the federal criminal defendant must actually have committed the crimes to which he or she is pleading. The defendant will be required to testify concerning their admitted crimes in a detailed proceeding, discussed in Federal Sentencing, unlike state and municipal criminal pleas in which the defendant may only be required to state the plea entered, i.e. Guilty or No Contest.

Upon entering a plea of guilty, a federal criminal defendant gives up many rights, including the government being required to prove their guilt beyond a reasonable doubt to a unanimous jury. Additionally, the federal criminal defendant consents to being sentenced by the federal judge presiding over their case.

Prior to a plea being entered, the United States Attorney's Office may agree with the federal criminal defense attorney to not recommend an enhanced sentence; however, the federal judge presiding over the case has sole authority to determine the defendant's sentence.

The most important preparation by the defendant's criminal defense attorney in a federal criminal case occurs after entering a plea, if the defendant forfeits his or her right to trial.

9th Step – Evaluating Litigating Your Federal Case

There are four primary resources available to a federal criminal defense attorney to fight your case: detention hearing, preliminary hearing, motion hearing, and jury trial. The detention hearing was discussed previously; therefore, this section will focus on the remaining tools to fight your case.

10th Step - Preliminary Hearing

Sometimes, but not always, the presiding judge will hold a preliminary hearing. Similar to the Grand Jury proceeding, the federal prosecutor will be required to show sufficient evidence exists to charge the defendant with the crimes to which he or she is pleading. This right belongs to the defendant and can be waived.

Additionally, the preliminary hearing must be held within 14 days if the federal criminal defendant is in custody, or within 21 days of initial appearance if the federal criminal defendant is out of custody.

Federal court preliminary hearings are similar to state court preliminary hearings. The Assistant United States Attorney, the prosecutor, will call witnesses and present evidence. Additionally, your federal criminal defense attorney can cross-examine and impeach the prosecutor's witnesses. However, unlike state court, the Assistant United States Attorney can introduce some evidence regardless of objection by your federal criminal defense attorney.

At the conclusion of the Assistant United States Attorney's presenting evidence, similar to state court preliminary hearings, the judge will decide if probable cause exists that the criminal defendant committed a crime. Trial will be held in the near future, if probable cause is found, or the judge will dismiss the case if he/she believes probable cause does not exist.

11th Step - Motion Practice

There is a wide range of issues, both legal and factual, that warrant federal criminal defense attorneys to seek relief by filing motions in federal court. Many of those may result in the suppression of evidence, or clarification on what will and will not be allowed to transpire in your jury trial.

Once you and your federal criminal defense attorney have processed the evidence and information in your case, you should discuss what issues and motions should be considered and filed in your case. Some of the most common motions filed in federal court, include: suppression, motions in limine, severance motions, and requests for procedural relief.

The effect of pre-trial motions in federal criminal trial include: courtroom, the defendant, evidence, witnesses, testimony, and the trial itself. Some of the most commonly litigated pre-trial motions in federal criminal trial are often variants of the following:

Motion to Dismiss: federal criminal defense attorneys can seek to dismiss the case for a lack of evidence or illegal search & seizure issues by federal investigators.

Motion to Suppress: federal criminal defense attorneys can seek to suppress or keep out evidence information, testimony, or witnesses, which is improper for a variety of reasons.

Motion for Change of Venue: federal criminal defense attorneys can seek to have a federal criminal trial heard in another federal district for a variety of reasons, such as pretrial publicity or prejudice in the district in high profile cases.

Although some motions cannot be resolved until issues occur during trial, an experienced federal criminal defense attorney can gain laser focus on the issues at trial by seeking and obtaining left and right limits on a variety of issues from the judge overseeing federal criminal trial. It is important to hire an experienced criminal defense attorney for your federal criminal defense that has knowledge of the federal criminal process and defenses available in your case.

12th Step – Federal Criminal Trial

Federal criminal trial proceedings are similar to state court criminal trials. However, it is more formal, and the trial judge will rule on most issues in advance of trial. In federal criminal trials, your defense attorney may or may not be allowed to question potential jurors.

In federal criminal trials, the U.S. Attorney or prosecutor must prove you are guilty beyond a reasonable doubt to a unanimous jury, just as District Attorneys must prove your guilt in state court jury trials. The preparation of your federal criminal defense attorney and his/her ability to impeach the prosecution's case and tell your story plays a major role in your chances for success.

As discussed above, the amount of evidence available for review in a federal criminal case is often a massive amount of information, and it is important that your attorney reviews and understands all the evidence in the government's possession. Many important decisions will take place during your trial, even in federal court, which is part of the reason why it is very important to work with an experienced federal criminal defense attorney to assist you in making those decisions.

Among the important decisions is whether or not to testify in your case. It is your right and your right alone to testify or not testify. The decision cannot be used against you by the prosecution or the jury. This decision, among many others, should be made with the advice of experienced federal criminal defense counsel.

In addition to deciding the law and evidence admissible at trial, the federal judge will decide the law to instruct the jury on; the jury instructions. This decision will dictate what the jury must find in order to decide the verdict, and how to consider the evidence. Your federal criminal defense attorney's ability to argue jury instructions' plays a large role in the success of your case.

Closing argument is the last chance for your federal criminal defense attorney to argue your case and the prosecution's failure to prove your guilt beyond a reasonable doubt. The prosecutor will be able to argue the government's case as well.

The final and most important part of your federal criminal trial is jury deliberation. During deliberations, the jury is charged with reaching a unanimous verdict, the jury must all vote for your guilt or you will not be convicted. Upon a verdict of not guilty, a federal criminal defendant is allowed to go home and go on with their life. However, upon conviction, post-conviction proceedings begin.

13th Step – Federal Sentencing

Whether your federal criminal case is resolved by your entry of a plea or following a guilty verdict at trial, unless your case is dismissed, you will proceed to sentencing in federal court. Federal sentencing consists of a very complex analysis, established by Congress, which sets minimum and maximum sentences for many crimes which federal judges use in attempting to find and determine a proper sentence.

U.S. Probation plays a major role in sentencing in federal court. After a plea or guilty verdict, the probation officer will conduct a presentence investigation or PSI to look into the background of the defendant, including a massive amount of information on your background. Once the PSI is completed, both your defense attorney and the prosecutor have an opportunity to object to the PSI, but once it is final, the case moves onto preparations for the sentencing hearing.

Prior to federal sentencing hearings, the parties may file a sentencing memorandum, to present arguments and issues to the sentencing judge. At the sentencing hearing, the Court will first evaluate the federal sentencing guidelines and then hear evidence and argument from all parties. The sentencing guidelines are advisory to the Court and set a recommended range of punishment in every case.

Your chosen defense attorney again has the opportunity to artfully tell your story and the circumstances of your case that warrant leniency in your sentence. Many aggravating factors and mitigating factors are considered by the judge and your defense attorney's ability to advocate for you plays a direct role in the outcome of your sentence.

14th Step – Beyond Sentencing

Even after your federal criminal case is complete, you still have options. You can choose to comply with the terms of your sentence, including supervision by U.S. Probation, and work to ensure you complete the process and can move on with your life. Alternatively, you can appeal a ruling or the entirety of your case.

The terms of your period of supervised release, after or instead of prison, will vary in every case. It is important to maintain good communication with your probation officer in order to stay in compliance. Failure to comply with the terms of your supervised release can result in your being sentenced to prison.

You have a right to file an appeal after the conclusion of your case, if you are not satisfied with the outcome or a legal ruling in your case. There are very specific timelines that must be complied with in order to effectuate your appeal. The first step is filing a notice of intent to appeal and identifying the records you will need for the appeal. Once this timeline starts, you will be required to submit your brief and other documents by the established timelines. You must work with an experienced federal criminal appeals attorney if you want to seek relief on appeal.

FEDERAL SENTENCING & BEYOND

"I highly recommend Mr. Cannon. He is professional, knowledgeable, trustworthy, works in a timely manner, and cares about his clients. In times of such hardship and vulnerability he is the kind of person you want in your corner. We had a previous lawyer who was horrible in every way possible. Working with John was a completely different experience."

Desiree

Federal crimes are enumerated, listed, in United States Code, which contains the statutory federal law in the United States. The majority of federal crimes are listed in Title 18 United States Code; however, almost every Title of the United States Code contains one or more criminal provisions.

Part of the logic behind the creation of Federal Sentencing Guidelines is uniformity in punishment. The Federal Judiciary, particularly the U.S. Sentencing Commission (discussed in the next section), wanted to correct the injustice of a federal criminal defendant in one federal district receiving a punishment far longer or shorter than a federal criminal defendant charged with the same offense in another part of the United States. Although the system still has disparity between Federal Districts, a federal criminal offender in the Western District of Oklahoma will now face a punishment similar to an offender in any District.

Brief History of Federal Sentencing

At the time of enactment, the Federal Sentencing Guidelines were mandatory, meaning federal judges were required to follow the exact framework of the guidelines. However, in 2005 the United States Supreme Court decided *United States v. Booker,* 543 U.S. 220 (2005), which found the mandatory prong of the Guidelines was not Constitutional.

Although the guidelines results are no longer mandatory, federal judges must perform the calculations in the Federal Sentencing Guidelines and consider the result in determining a federal criminal defendant's sentence. Additionally, federal judges will consider a Presentence Report, which paints a picture of the defendant and the charges.

How Federal Sentencing Guidelines Work

The Federal Sentencing Guidelines are just what they sound like – a guide to sentencing federal criminal offenders. Most, but not all, federal criminal offenses are listed in one of the forty-three (43) Offense Levels.

Additionally, each federal criminal offender is assigned one of the six Criminal History Categories. The criminal history categories are based on the offender's criminal history: specifically, the seriousness of their history and how recently the offense occurred. Imaged as a graph; the Offense Level is the Y-axis and the Criminal History Category is the X-axis. The overlap or intersection of the two axes (Offense level x Criminal History Category) determines the federal criminal offender's range of punishment.

Each Guideline Range is separated by six (6) months incarceration or 25 percent, whichever is greater. Judges are now advised, previously required as discussed above, to choose a sentence within the Guideline Range, unless a factor convinces the federal judge a different sentence is appropriate.

U.S. Sentencing Commission

The Federal sentencing guidelines are written and maintained by an independent federal agency, called the United States Sentencing Commission, a federal agency that is part of the federal judicial branch. The United States Sentencing Commission (https://ussc.gov/) analyzes criminal sentencing information and consults other branches of government on policies that affect criminal issues.

Offense Levels: Seriousness of Federal Crime

In addition to the sentencing analysis discussed in the last section, forty-three (43) offense seriousness levels exist. You are correct in assuming the higher the number the more serious the federal offense, i.e. First-Degree Murder has a base offense level of 43 (the highest level). The final offense level is set by taking the Base Level, explained in the last section and adding or subtracting based on the offense characteristics.

What Can Raise or Lower Offense Level?

I. Raising the Offense Level

Specific federal offenses usually carry a number of Offense Characteristics. The characteristics can increase or decrease the base offense level, which plays a role in the federal sentence received by an offender. The following are some of the most common level adjustments:

Crimes motivated by hate or knowledge that the victim was unusually vulnerable

- Obstruction of justice or multiple prior convictions
- Property loss greater than $2,500 adds one level
- Property loss greater than $10,000 adds two levels
- Property loss greater than $800,000 adds five levels
- Displaying a firearm in a robbery adds five levels– Discharge of a firearm in a robbery adds seven levels
- Violence and/or great financial loss will increase levels

Now that you are familiar with some of the offense characteristics that increase the base offense level; the next section illustrates Offense Characteristics that decrease the base offense level.

II. Lowering the Offense

Some Offense Characteristics lower the offense level. The following characteristics are the most common that lower, or decrease, the base offense level:

- Substantial Assistance to authorities, (discussed below)
- Participation in an early disposition program
- Victim's conduct that significantly contributes to the offense
- Lesser harm, (discussed below)

Federal Sentencing Adjustments

Adjustments are another factor in federal criminal sentencing. They potentially apply to any offense, and will either increase or decrease the offense level. There are three categories of Adjustments: victim-related; offender role; and obstruction of justice. Minimal participation can decrease the base level by four levels. However, obstruction or a crime involving a vulnerable victim will increase the offense level.

Multiple Count: a federal criminal defendant convicted on multiple counts, i.e. more than one federal offense, will receive one "Combined Offense Level for all the crimes. The guidelines begin with the most serious offense and all other offenses will either increase or not affect the offense level.

Acceptance of Responsibility: the judge may reduce the offense level by two levels for a federal criminal defendant taking or accepting responsibility for the offense. Upon a motion by the prosecution, stating the defendant's early guilty plea avoided U.S. Attorney and court resources, the judge may decrease the offense level by an additional level, if the offense level is at sixteen (16) or higher.

Although federal judges have discretion in applying the downward adjustment, the following factors should be considered: criminal Defendant's truthful admission of participation in a crime, restitution to the victim before a guilty verdict; and/or entering a guilty plea.

Criminal History: As in state criminal proceedings, the offender's criminal record plays a large role in the guidelines. One of the Six (6) Criminal History Categories discussed above will be set based upon the length and how recent previous crimes occurred. Many first-time federal offenders are placed in Criminal History Category One, the lowest category, based on having minimal or no criminal record. Alternatively, criminal offenders with substantial criminal records will be assigned a higher Criminal History Category.

Departures from the Federal Guidelines

Understandably, the Federal Sentencing Guideline point federal defendants are most concerned with is downward departures. This final step in the sentencing analysis is required pursuant to 18 U.S.C. Section 3553(b). The federal judge must determine whether or not aggravating or mitigating factors are applicable, which would support making the offense deserving a lesser punishment that the U.S. Sentencing Commission failed to consider or failed to give sufficient weight or importance. Federal judges may impose a sentence above or below the guidelines, if he or she determines an aggravating or mitigation circumstance exists and memorializes the reasoning in writing.

Fortunately, federal criminal defendants can appeal if the federal judge imposes an upward departure. Unfortunately, the U.S. Attorney's Office may appeal, if the federal judge grants a downward departure. The most famous departure is the Substantial Assistance Departure.

In state court criminal proceedings, cooperation with prosecutors or law enforcement may result in a benefit in your state court criminal proceedings. Likewise, in federal criminal proceedings this downward departure, reduction in prison sentence, may be applied for substantially assisting in the investigation and/or prosecution of another, usually more serious, federal criminal offender.

Federal criminal defense attorneys may not request the Substantial Assistance Departure, only the federal prosecutor can. However, an experienced federal criminal defense attorney can solidify your receiving such a request by the prosecution, if you provide the proper assistance.

Finally, if your federal criminal defense attorney is able to convince the federal judge imposing sentence that following the guidelines would be unreasonable, the federal judge may grant a variance from the guidelines to your benefit. Again, the federal judge must state his or her basis for doing so in writing.

Downward Departure from the Guidelines

An artfully crafted argument by your federal criminal defense attorney may result in additional downward departure. The following are some of the most common downward departure factors:

Victim's Conduct (Section 5K2.10) when a victim contributes to the significance of a federal criminal offense; a federal judge may depart downward on the sentence below the guidelines to reflect the aggravation by the victim. The federal sentencing judge should consider the following:

- The physical characteristics of the victim, in comparison with the defendant;
- The victim's conduct, and efforts, if any by the defendant to prevent confrontation;
- The danger reasonably perceived by the defendant;
- The actual danger to the defendant by the victim;

- Any other conduct by the victim affecting the danger presented; The reasonableness of the defendant's response to the victim's conduct.

Lesser Harm (Section 5k2.11) when a federal criminal defendant commits a federal crime to avoid a believed greater harm; a federal judge may depart downward on the sentence, if the circumstances diminish the interest in punishing the conduct.

Coercion or Duress (Section 5K2.12) when a federal criminal – defendant commits a federal crime under duress, fear, or blackmail, but it is not a complete defense; a federal judge may depart downward on the sentence.

Diminished capacity (Section 5K2.13) when a federal criminal – defendant commits a federal crime with diminished mental capacity, which contributed to the commission of the offense; a federal judge may depart downward on the sentence. However, voluntary intoxication and other factors may negate this basis for a downward departure.

Voluntary Disclosure (Section 5K2.16) when a federal criminal – defendant admits an offense, which would likely not have been discovered otherwise; a federal judge may depart downward on the sentence.

Aberrant Behavior (Section 5K2.20) when a federal criminal – defendant commits a federal crime that did not involve planning, was of limited duration; and is a deviation from the defendant's otherwise law-abiding life; a federal judge may depart downward on the sentence for policy reasons. However, this does not apply in the case of serious bodily injury; the use of a firearm; or serious drug trafficking.

Punishment Zones

There are four federal sentencing zones, set ranges of length of incarceration. A defendant in the lowest of the four zones is eligible for federal probation, i.e. no imprisonment. Further, pursuant to U.S.S.G. Section 5C1.1(c)(3), a federal sentencing judge may create a combination of conditions, including, but not limited to home detention and community confinement. Federal defendants in the third highest zone may receive split sentences, i.e. serve only half of their sentence incarcerated.

This topic leads to the consideration of Federal Criminal Probation.

Federal Criminal Probation

The Federal Sentencing Guidelines limit probation to specific circumstances. Probation without any confinement is limited to Zone A, sentencing ranges six months and below, as discussed above. Section 5B1.3 of the Sentencing Guidelines sets out statutorily required and discretionary conditions. The mandatory conditions include:

- Not committing any crimes
- Not possessing illegal drugs
- Perform community service and pay restitution
- Submit to drug testing, unless suspended by the judge
- Advise the court of any change in financial circumstances
- Comply with sex offender registration, if applicable
- Computer limitations by sex offenders, if applicable
- Submit to DNA testing

Forms of Confinement

The Federal Sentencing Guidelines list four (4) forms of confinement, which may be imposed as part of probation. 1) community confinement; 2) home detention; 3) shock incarceration; and 4) intermittent confinement.

Community confinement includes circumstances such as a halfway house. Home detention, as implied, is supervision from home with the ability to go to work, school, community service work, or out for personal needs. Intermittent confinement is periods of being in custody and out of custody. Shock incarceration is a boot camp, which was discontinued years ago.

In order to facilitate re-entry to the community, federal courts impose supervised release after confinement. Unless statutorily required, federal judges have discretion to waive supervised release. Chapter Seven (7) of the Federal Sentencing Guidelines lays out the penalty for violating the conditions of probation or supervised release, which may include incarceration.

Federal criminal sentencing, and the Federal Sentencing Guidelines, are a highly technical area of criminal law. Federal judges strictly enforce the fast-paced and detailed procedures that govern these cases. Federal prosecutors are hard-lined, highly experienced trial attorneys. Therefore, your chosen federal criminal defense attorney must be experienced with federal criminal procedure and be a skilled advocate.

In order to intelligently decide the multiple issues you will face during the course of your federal criminal prosecution, you need an experienced and Fierce Advocate® You should contact an experienced federal criminal defense attorney as early as possible in your federal criminal prosecution. It is my hope this page has educated you on major issues in Federal Sentencing Guidelines.

MILITARY CRIMINAL DEFENSE OVERVIEW

"Even though he wasn't able to take my case because I'm from Texas and he is from OK he was so kind and helpful, he still had the time to answer any questions I had and offer to send me information about another lawyer in my state."

Itzel

Informed Criminal Defense

As a Judge Advocate and private military defense attorney, I am tasked with defending Service Members through a wide range of legal processes and procedures that make up our military justice system. The military must operate in environments across the world, which requires commanders to conduct military justice actions during combat or any other environment. Due to the varied responsibilities of military commanders in dealing with infractions, the tools available to commanders vary from employment consequences to administrative actions and the spectrum of criminal prosecution.

At the least serious end of the spectrum, administrative actions exist to address minor infractions, more related to employment issues than criminal issues. These actions include: counseling statements, evaluations; Officer Evaluation Reports or Non-Commissioned Officer Evaluation Reports; and Reprimands.

These actions are initiated by a supervisor or commander and can have negative implications on a Soldier's career or finances. Service members have limited due process rights in these proceedings; however, experienced counsel can facilitate crafting and presenting rebuttals, letters of support, and may communicate with your commander's JAG, or commander directly, on your behalf.

The middle level of consequences is administrative actions, which make up the bulk of the military actions. Administrative military justice procedures have more serious consequences than the previous level discussed and include the following: removal from promotion lists; reduction in rank; withdrawal of federal recognition; non-judicial punishment, and a variety of other actions, each with its own unique procedure, regulations, and level of due process. These actions require the assistance of an experienced military defense attorney to protect your interests in continued military service.

The broad category of administrative actions can have serious implications; however, none of these actions can result in confinement. You need an advocate on your side, outside of the command structure, to ensure the process you are facing is followed precisely and you are afforded the maximum opportunity to receive the best outcome.

Finally, the criminal justice end of the spectrum, which is most similar to the state and federal criminal justice systems discussed above. Potential outcomes of all military justice actions include confinement and/or receiving a federal conviction. The potential for confinement or imprisonment is in addition to the other negative impacts in military justice, such as continued income, retirement, rank, and hard labor.

Federal service members are held to the Uniform Code of Military Justice (UCMJ), found in U.S. Code Title 10. National Guard soldiers are held to their individual States' code, if they are in a non-federal status. Oklahoma National Guard Soldiers are under the Oklahoma Military Justice Code (OCMJ) and Oklahoma Statutes title 44.

Actions under the UCMJ are criminal in nature and result in one of three levels of Court-Martial actions: summary, special, or general. It is equally important to work with an experienced military criminal defense attorney in any of these actions, as it is to hire experienced counsel for state or federal criminal defense. The rules and procedures are complex in military justice and only a few attorneys in any location practice in this area. It is important to identify and hire the right attorney to protect your interests.

MILITARY ADMINISTRATIVE PROCEEDINGS OVERVIEW

"John is one impressive attorney who is super knowledgeable, quick witted, confident, passionate and a true advocate for all clients. He has a heart for military clients and helped me get involved in the Veteran Diversion Group. He gave me the best advice and you can not go wrong with this group. Literally, once my case finally got charged, the case was closed within 2 months. Yes, I said CLOSED (charges dismissed) The credit is truly due to John Cannon & Tom Stone's knowledge. Thank you so very much to everyone involved in handling my case. Also a special shout out to Brittany who helped with my case."

Stephen

When a commander determines that your continued military service is not beneficial to his or her formation, commanders will often initiate administrative separation proceedings, which can result in the end of your military career and a negative discharge characterization. Being separated from the military and the characterization of service you receive when separated from the military can and will have lasting effects on your employment opportunities, retirement and Department of Veterans Affairs benefits, finances, and potentially confinement.

This gray area between being punished in the military and criminal prosecution is very serious and requires working with experienced military defense counsel to increase the likelihood of a positive outcome. Each branch of the military has regulations that dictate the basis, procedure, and due process involved for each type of separation, from Court-Martial to retirement. Cannon & Associates can assist you and ensure your rights are protected and the proper procedure is followed in your military justice case.

Your Rights prior to Separation from the Military

You are entitled to a defense in any military administrative action. However, your rights depend on a number of factors, including your years of service and the seriousness of the consequence you are facing. In a separation action, you are entitled to the following:

- Your Right to an Administrative Board, if you have more than 6 years of qualifying service
- Right to submit a conditional waiver (military justice version of an offer/plea agreement)
- Right to request witnesses on your behalf
- Notice of the specific separation action
- Basis of your separation action
- Notice of the least favorable characterization of discharge you can receive
- Notice of the characterization of service your commander recommends
- Right to speak to a military defense attorney
- Right to submit matters and evidence on your behalf
- Right to request a Board, and counsel to represent you in a number of these Chapters
- Right to an Administrative Board, if your commander is recommending an Other than Honorable (OTH) or Bad Conduct Discharge (BCD)

CONCLUSION ON MILITARY ACTIONS

Military justice and court-martial practice is similar to federal criminal trials; however, there are unique procedural circumstances that make military justice a field of its own. The Military Rules of Evidence are based on the Federal Rules of Evidence, and members hear evidence that is admitted to decide on rendering the accused's guilt or not. There are three levels of court-martial, with differing levels of procedural protections and rights based upon the level of possible negative consequences.

The complexity of the procedures and understanding of the pain points of commanders, what they are looking for in an outcome, makes military defense work a very specific field of work. In order to seek the best possible outcome, you must know what commanders care about in your case or court-martial. When you can identify the issue the commander cares about most, it is often possible to obtain a better outcome than, if you face the matter alone.

As in civilian criminal proceedings, negotiations take place, as well as motion practice to protect client's interests and their defense. As is the case in any area of law, it is vital to work with an experienced attorney that is well versed in the legal issues and process you are facing.

Cannon & Associates

YOUR FIERCE ADVOCATES®

"Mr. Cannon represented my husband on a case we were very concerned might not go our way. The next court date we were predicting my husband might not be coming home for a while. Not only did Mr. Cannon and his office team work quickly on the matter, they all were extremely informative and communicated well with us through the whole process. Once in court, Mr. Cannon communicated thoroughly with us, went over our options & possibilities, and didn't give up fighting for my husband's innocence. He was able to get the case dismissed for my husband. It was truly a blessing to have someone work hard for our family and care to make sure he stayed home with us. The office has been great working with us on payments in order for them to keep representing our case. Overall, we were beyond impressed with the work done and would highly recommend Mr. Cannon and his office for anyone needing a great attorney."

Stefanie

Informed Criminal Defense

The Fierce Advocates® at Cannon & Associates take a team approach to every client we have the honor of serving. We have an amazing staff of defense attorneys, paralegals, administrative staff, and investigators that will fight for you and your family!

We meet as a complete team once every single week in our weekly Case Strategy Meeting to develop a plan to reach the best outcome possible for every client by masterminding every case as a team. When you work with Cannon & Associates, you do not get one defense attorney, you are represented by our entire team and your case is strategized by everyone from the most experienced attorneys and investigators to the newest members of our team that often have some of the best ideas!

If you or your loved one are currently facing or potentially facing criminal charges, now is the right moment to hire an experienced criminal defense attorney. No matter where you are in the process, it is never too early to be represented by experienced criminal defense counsel. By early intervention into your case, a criminal defense team can capture witness statements, conduct an independent investigation for your defense, and secure evidence, such as camera footage and social media messages before they are lost forever!

You cannot change the past, but a great attorney and defense team can help you change your FUTURE. Without an experienced criminal defense attorney you may dig yourself into a deeper hole without even knowing it. As discussed in previous chapters, police and investigators will not tell you that you are providing them more for their investigation against you until it is too late, or never.

How you handle the investigation in your case may dictate the outcome and whether or not your case is dismissed or you serve time. You need more than a criminal defense attorney, you need a Fierce Advocate® with a range of experience, a track record of success for clients, and the respect of prosecutors and the bench.

It is never too early to hire the right criminal defense attorney if you have been arrested or believe you are under investigation. Even a suspicion of being investigated is cause to hire an experienced defense attorney. The expense of hiring an experienced criminal defense attorney may assist you in avoiding criminal charges or reduced charging. Whether you are able to avoid charges all together or must defend your criminal case, investing in working with the best criminal defense team you can is an investment into your future!

It is not cheap to hire the right criminal defense attorney; however, it is far more expensive to your future and freedom, if you do not hire the right criminal defense attorney. Without a great criminal defense attorney, you are likely to face the following expenses:

Burdensome probation terms

Expensive probation fees

Expensive court costs and fines

Probation classes that take you away from work and family

Treatment options that are expensive and time consuming

Being away from your family and work, if you are forced to serve jail or even prison time

Not only is hiring a great criminal defense attorney an INVESTMENT in your future, it may also directly save you thousands by avoiding the unnecessary expenses listed above.

The exercise of your right to hire a qualified and experienced criminal defense attorney can never be used against you in an investigation or court. Further, it offers benefits throughout the investigative phase of your case that you would not have without an experienced attorney.

Although you cannot control whether or not you will be arrested or charged, you do have some control over the process by hiring an experienced criminal defense attorney. It is the wisest choice you can make when facing the justice system.

CANNON & ASSOCIATES: SET APART

"The team at Cannon and Associates have been very helpful and professional. They have kept me up to date on matters and have helped in guiding me the right direction to move forward."

Garth

Few criminal defense attorneys have handled the number and caliber of criminal cases that I have in my career to this point. However, that is not the only reason to consider hiring my Firm. My clients benefit every day from the way in which I conduct business and my dedication to every client throughout the particular process they are facing.

We are constantly striving to reach the best possible outcome for every client, through Fierce Advocacy and dedication to each individual client's case. Every client we represent, from a simple possession of drugs to Murder in the First Degree, deserves and receives dedicated, detail-oriented service from our Firm.

We consider representing a client be an honor and responsibility, which our firm takes very seriously. We treat every client and potential client as a person with a life beyond their case, with hopes and dreams beyond their current circumstance. Our analysis of your case does not begin with or end with your charges, it is about you: your past, your present, and your future.

We are dedicated to identifying clients' greatest fears and finding a way to protect clients from that fear becoming their reality. We cannot obtain every goal for every client, but we strive to ensure every client understands every step of the process and feels their desires are respected, which is our central focus in representing that client. Our Firm strives to be attorney and counselor at law. You are more than a number and a criminal case at our Firm, you are our client, and we will walk beside you every step of the way, fight for you, and answer every question along the way in order to be Your Fierce Advocates®.

We hope this book has answered many of the questions and concerns you and your family are facing with a pending criminal investigation or charges in Oklahoma. At the least, this book should have opened your eyes to issues and factors in your matter that you need to keep in mind throughout the process and got you thinking about the questions you should be asking along the way.

Whether you work with our team or not, we hope this book will help you in making a well-informed decision in hiring an experienced criminal defense law firm. Your future, your freedom, and your reputation rely heavily upon the defense team you work with on your case. Please take the time to find the right defense for you.

We wish you and yours the best in this process and beyond. Please let us know, if we can be of assistance. You have more control than you think you do in the outcome of your case. Understand the process and follow the sound advice of a good criminal defense attorney. If we are the right fit for you, we would be honored to be Your Fierce Advocates®.

ACKNOWLEDGEMENTS

"Everyone at this firm is outstanding! Very Professional and Respectful People! From the very beginning they treated me with Respect and took my case serious! The outcome for me was better than I ever expected!!"

Kenneth

We would like to express our gratitude to you for taking the time to read this book and educate yourself with *Informed Criminal Defense*. Our firm is passionate about being Fierce Advocates® for the clients and families we have the privilege to serve. You have taken the first step to the rest of your life and **Your Better Future Now.**

I am thankful for a deep and profound faith in God, which continually shapes my life and how I try to interact with the world. My amazing wife, Megan. She is a bright light in my life, my inspiration, and is always there to support me and our family. Thank you to my three beautiful children, you bring so much joy to the world and remind me every day why it is so important to fight for the benefit and happiness of children in family court.

To the amazing team in our office that works for the benefit of our clients day in and day out, you change lives for the better.

Informed Criminal Defense

CLIENT TESTIMONIALS

"EXCELLENT law firm, HIGHLY recommend. You can't beat the expertise of John Cannon! When we called the office for help Shelley, Angelia, and Kelly were very compassionate and professional during the intake process. After obtaining detailed information to identify what our specific legal needs were, we were quoted a price and payment options. It was determined which Attorney would best suit our situation and we were paired up with the Attorney's Paralegal to get things started. Brittany/Paralegal was excellent, kind, communicative and responsive to all of our needs and inquiries. John Cannon was articulate, informative, and handled the case like the amazing PRO that he is! He is definitely a "Who's Who" of attorneys in the State of Oklahoma. Thank you so much to Mr. Cannon and the entire professional Team that stands behind him. Don't hesitate to call this law firm and let them help you navigate the best way and best attorney within the firm to handle your legal situation!

Kathy

Mr. Cannon has represented me on 2 criminal cases and one civil case over the past 4 years. He has always served me honestly, speedily and with good moral direction. John has integrity and humility. He has never belittled me or treated me in an unfair manner. I appreciate all that he has done for me and I most certainly recommend him to family, strangers and friends. I will definitely use Mr. Cannon in the future for any and all of my family's legal matters."

Candice

"John is a highly respected attorney. Professional and compassionate. He has a wealth of knowledge, being a military officer and having served as an Assistant District Attorney, a Public Defender, and an Assistant Attorney General. He helped a friend's son who was headed down the wrong path, but through John's legal defense the young man is now a successful business owner."

Attorney Colleague

"John Cannon is an amazing attorney. During one of the most difficult times of my life he showed compassion, was honest, and patiently answered my questions."

Sharon

"John is a very professional attorney, who is not only concerned about the welfare of his client but very attentive and considerate of the family, or other bodies that are in the face of the adversity. While working on my family member's case, John took time out to take a class that would educate him on how to approach the many different types of cases tried in the court room. John proved his sincerity to the calling of his job, being an attorney. I would definitely recommend him to anyone."

Laquita

"Mr. Cannon went above and beyond for my wife. She was facing some pretty hard fines and prison time with the US Marshals. Mr. Cannon fought a hard fight and got her a GREAT offer. Words cannot express how much I appreciate him and what he did for my wife. I would give 10 stars and I will be promoting him. He's that awesome. He keeps you informed, he will text or call you back, and he goes above what he is asked to do and I can reassure you. HE WILL FIGHT FOR YOU OR YOUR FAMILY MEMBER. I will continue retaining him for other things my wife is battling. High five and a great big hug to Mr. Cannon. Thank you!!! John took the reins and provided us instant peace of mind. He was timely, respectful, transparent, very professional, honest and courteous. The service he provided was above and beyond our expectations. Can't believe professionals like him are around. Highly highly without reservations recommend him and his team."

Tara

ABOUT THE AUTHOR

The Founder of Cannon & Associates, John Cannon is a family man and dedicated to service. He is blessed to work with an amazing team that serves its community every day. John is also a serving JAG officer in the Oklahoma Army National Guard and a combat veteran.

John has defended Soldiers in all aspects of the military justice system in a reserve and active-duty status. He has tried Court-Martial and other military justice actions on multiple installations, including Fort Sill, Tinker Air Force Base, Vance Air Force Base, and Fort Bragg. Additionally, he represented soldiers during active-duty service in Washington, D.C.

He continues to serve as the Brigade Judge Advocate for the 45th Field Artillery Brigade and has advised and represented countless soldiers in all types of criminal and administrative actions.

John has received numerous peer nominated and reviewed awards, including: The National Trial Lawyers 40 under 40 Award in Criminal Defense and holds the Super Lawyer designation. He and the team at Cannon & Associates pride themselves at being Fierce Advocates® for every client they serve.

Our team strives to give every client all the information available at every step of their case to ensure each and every client understands his or her options before any important decision.

Finally, we wish you and yours the very best in this difficult time and we are ready and willing to meet with you for a free completely confidential consultation to discuss your case and the next step in defending your case and freedom.

Made in the USA
Columbia, SC
21 May 2023